WITCHES

By the same Author

GOGMAGOG: THE BURIED GODS
GHOST AND GHOUL

Witches

BY T. C. LETHBRIDGE

The Citadel Press
Secaucus, New Jersey

Third paperbound printing, 1972
Copyright © 1962 by T. C. Lethbridge
All rights reserved
Published by Citadel Press, Inc.
A subsidiary of Lyle Stuart, Inc.
120 Enterprise Ave., Secaucus, N.J. 07094
Manufactured in the United States of America
ISBN 0-8065-0286-X

Contents

Figures

vii

Preface

There is really only one study of man, and this should be known as Anthropology. Medical Science, History, Archaeology, Folk Lore and the rest are all branches of the one study. But this present age is one of specialization and all these branches are tending to become so elaborate and, at the same time, so constricted that we are in need of trained middle-men, who have a wide enough grasp of all of them to be able to pull the whole thing together and present it in readable form to those who wish to learn. These middle-men really do not exist today, for there is no training to fit them for the task. The Scottish university system is much better than the English in this respect; but even there the scope of training could be wider.

After watching the steady growth of specialization for many years, sometimes when sitting in considerable boredom on a Faculty Board at Cambridge, it seemed to me to be something of a duty to spend as much time as possible trying to pull together some of the information which is being scattered among different studies. To this I add my own ideas and speculations, in the hope that the resulting pottage may be of general interest and even perhaps of some value.

As I sit at my desk here in Branscombe and look over my left shoulder, I can see the sea through a gap in the wooded ridges. Sometimes fog shrouds it and at other times it is blotted out by driving squalls of wind and rain. But all the time I know that it is there and with that knowledge I am content.

For several thousand years that sea has been the only road by which men and ideas could come to Britain and the very crossing of that sea has always carried an element of risk and change. No idea has ever come to rest in Britain which has not been changed in the process, and it has been the same with religious ideas as much as with any others. Therefore we must not expect to find that our old concepts were exactly the same as they were on the continent of Europe. We must also find that we have to experience a certain amount of discomfort if we are to learn about them at all. The discomfort in this study lies in the inordinate number of unfamiliar names with which we have to cope. I know that these may be boring to readers and I would avoid the use of them if I could, but it is impossible. I have reduced them as far as I dare to do so. But, just as in the seaman's trade it is necessary to learn a new, but simple and effective, list of words, so this is necessary in the study of an old religion to compare it with others. For this comparison one must use the names of the gods and goddesses which belong to them. Therefore no apology is really needed and if readers find these names difficult and boring they must understand that I have done my best to simplify matters. I am the last person to introduce unnecessary names or terms. I leave these when possible to pedagogues.

I need not say much more by way of introduction. The witches themselves have been kind and helpful; but, after hundreds of years of persecution, no one ought to expect them to give themselves away. I have deliberately avoided prying into secrets which they may wish to keep. The subject, however, is of great general interest and in many ways I think they have been wickedly wronged. No study of religious history in Britain can be even approximately correct which does not attempt to evaluate their beliefs. They obviously represent the oldest form of rationalized religion which still exists. One can hardly describe totemistic beliefs as rational.

With this introductory warning, let us cut the cackle and come to the horses; there are many in this story.

My wife, as on many former occasions, has been of the greatest help with this study. I think she has found it more interesting than most of my efforts and perhaps this is some slight recompense for her hard work in typing it out.

T.C.L.

'Diana and her darling crew shall pluck your
        fingers fine,
And lead you forth right pleasantly to sup the
        honey wine.
To sup the honey wine, my loves, and breathe
        the heavenly air,
And dance, as the young angels dance. Ah god
        that I were there!'

(Apparently a sixteenth-century version of a
hymn to Diana. It is sung to the tune of 'Jerusalem my happy home', a tune which may well
have belonged to it in the first place.)

Chapter One

THIS book is an exercise in deduction and this exercise was undertaken in an attempt to form a clear picture in my mind from the information which I have been collecting for the past four years or so. It is deduction applied to an old religion instead of to a criminal act. Most of the evidence is circumstantial, or inferential, and can neither be proved nor disproved. The results obtained in the book may be quite wrong, but they make sense to me and may perhaps have some entertainment value to others. The clues are drawn from ancient literature, anthropology, archaeology and folk-lore, with the addition of information supplied by modern devotees of the witch cult. The theme is continued from the ideas suggested in *Gogmagog*.

Those who hope to find detailed accounts of poor old women mumbling over wax images in hovels, or pinning living frogs to bits of wood and dropping them into wells, will be disappointed. This is not a treatise on magic, but an investigation of old religious belief. Neither is any interest taken in the obscene decadence of the Black Mass and similar performances. These are not edifying in themselves and only remotely connected with the cult. As a Highland farmer once said to me, when describing the condition of a neighbour's house, 'There is a difference between dirt and filth.' This observation applies to the witch cult. Although its devotees performed rites which appear to be highly indecent in a modern context, these were done in the firm belief that they were the way in which their deities required to be worshipped and not in a licentious spirit. All witches aver that they derive a great sense of serenity and peace from their ceremonies, presumably as a result of psychological relaxation. The Black Mass is performed as a magic trick to obtain unlawful desires. The one is dirt today: the other is filth. Dirt can be washed off easily: filth is ingrained.

The main purpose of this book is to try to find out by reasoning and inference whether Dr. Margaret Murray's witch cult, which she resurrected from almost complete oblivion in her *Witch Cult in Western Europe* and *God of the Witches*, can be identified with an earlier belief. If it can, where did this belief come from and when did it arise? To do this, I am going to make use of any scraps of evidence which seem to fit into the picture, regardless of what subject produces them. There is fortunately little dogma as yet in the study of what may be called Palaeo-theology. The dogma will come no doubt, as it always does in any subject. The dogma formulated by Malinowski, that the anthropology of Europe was too difficult for study, has been a great hindrance to research and robbed his devotees of the most interesting area in the world. The techniques of the anthropologists are becoming so onerous that their range of vision is narrowing week by week. The dogmatic tail is wagging the anthropological dog and before long the technical tail will wag the archaeological dog also. The scholar degenerates into the artisan. There is nothing really wrong with these tails, only the dogs need more biscuits and a run now and then. One has seen exactly the same conditions develop in the field of zoology. There no young man dared to investigate reports of the discovery of some new animal, because his boss had said that such a thing could not exist. It was as much as the young man's job and livelihood were worth for him to show the slightest interest in the report. Few things exert a greater pressure than an empty belly! At the same time, these same zoologists were busy in museums creating numerous new species from dried skins and bones, despite the fact that observers in the field reported seeing all these new species happily breeding together. This phase of zoology appears to be on the wane after a series of shocks. Any day now we may see somebody wander into South Kensington Museum with a Loch Ness monster on a string. In anthropology and archaeology it is just getting into its stride and we must expect, for a generation or so, that the dicta of former heroes of these subjects will be followed with greater reverence than the Gospels. Elaboration in technique takes the place of enthusiastic investigation. Without controlled imagination, the result is partial paralysis, to say nothing of profound boredom.

Now, the witch cult still survives as an organized belief in

No. 887-17 Date July 11t 19 75

Name   L Erickson

Address   755-3268

SOLD BY	CASH	C. O. D.	CHARGE	ON ACCT.	MDSE. RETD.	PAID OUT	

QUAN.		DESCRIPTION	PRICE	AMOUNT	
1	1	Witches by Lethbridge		2	45
	2				13
	3				
	4			2	58
	5				
	6				
	7				
	8				
	9				
	10				
	11				
	12				

Customer's
Order No.

Rec'd
By

KEEP THIS SLIP FOR REFERENCE

5H 527 Rediform

England today. I have talked with members of witch covens. It is not possible to learn a great deal about its beliefs, or ritual, however, because it is a secret religion owing to the persecution it has undergone. To learn all, one would have to become a member of a coven and then it would not be possible to write about it owing to the oath of secrecy. Nevertheless a great body of information has been collected by Dr. Murray and others, while recently a practising member of a coven, Dr. G. B. Gardner, has published several books which lift some of the covering thrown over the subject.

Taking the information collected by the folk-lore enthusiasts, of whom the late Charles Leland was a notable example, together with the disclosures of the witches themselves, it is possible to form a very fair idea of the religion and to compare it with others. In the next chapter I intend to give a summary of what the religion appears to be, but first it is necessary to give a warning.

All religions without exception appear to go through periods of evolution and devolution. They also go through times of amalgamation with other beliefs and those of splitting up into sects. Some enlightened and often very great personality formulates and teaches a theory of the meaning of life and a code of ethics to go with this theory. The persons taught seldom, if ever, grasp the whole of his meaning and never remember all of it. A classic example of this is told of the convocation of Buddha's disciples soon after their master's death. One claimed to have learnt the whole thing by heart and recited what he remembered to the meeting. At once a second disciple rose and, saying that he never remembered Buddha teaching anything of the kind, stalked out of the assembly. From that moment two schools of thought were formed and have existed for well over two thousand years. If this does not happen at once, it is certain to occur later.

The next stage follows when the religion gathers impetus and former members of other cults join it. Some of these invariably bring parts of their earlier beliefs and add them to the master's teaching. A very little comparison between the teaching of Christ, as recorded in the Gospels, with the dogmas of the various branches of the Christian Church today, will show that much has been added to the original; while the early examples of the Creed are about half the length of the existing version.

3

Not only do converts bring fragments of their old faith into their new one, but directly a formal priesthood comes into existence it makes changes for its own benefit. Priests must eat and in normal circumstances they need clothes. The laity of their religion must be persuaded to provide these necessities. One of the first steps is to make it clear that the gods need edible sacrifices. These are offered to the gods and then, as the gods do not seem to want them, gobbled up by the priests. The man who first thought of this most ingenious idea deserved to succeed in his world of humbug. Before this can be done, however, it is necessary to make the rules of the religion so hard to understand that only a trained priest can perform the necessary ceremonies. Thus, by elevating themselves into a position of go-betweens, with the gods on the one hand and the laity on the other, they are secured of their food supply and such other materials as they can persuade their congregation to offer. Even a gypsy fortune-teller needs her hand to be crossed with silver before she will practise her art.

From time to time new thinkers and reformers come along to add their quota to the interpretations which have been placed on the original teaching. After a relatively short space of time the first master would find it hard to believe that all this had grown out of what he had once taught. There can be little doubt that Zoroaster, Krishna, Buddha and Christ would suffer from considerable alarm and despondency could they see (and who is to say that they do not see?) the often well-meaning distortions which have happened to their work.

It seems as though this distortion of original thought and the congealing of flexible teaching into rigid dogma, is the fate which awaits most of man's better ideas. Florence Nightingale revolutionized nursing. Her humane teaching hardened into such rigid rules of hospital routine that it needed two world wars to begin to loosen their grip. Branches of learning, fascinating in themselves, become encased in strait-jackets and the learned parrots who teach them bitterly resent the appearance of any innovator. The religious parrots of the past had a far firmer grip than is possible today, for there was no popular press or wireless to shake their grasp.

We should expect therefore an ancient religion, which had once got a firm hold, to differ widely from the teaching of its

4

founder by including all sorts of extraneous matter. At the same time, once it was really set in its way, it would take some fairly violent movement to change its dogma and ritual.

Remembering these points, we can now begin our study of the witch cult.

Chapter Two

IN 1899 Charles Leland published a small book entitled *Aradia, or The Gospel of the Witches*. This book appears to be rare and it seems probable that it was smothered in some way by vested interests. Leland was a most energetic collector of folklore in Italy. He maintained, apparently with justification, that much of what he had collected originated in a period before the rise of Roman civilization and that, amongst other things, he had resuscitated Etruscan customs and that the names of their gods were still remembered in Tuscany. This may have been too much for Victorian scholars to believe, despite the fact that the life of folk tradition is very long. Over a period of years I have learnt by painful experience that Victorian judgments on these matters are seldom to be relied on. Scarcely anything they said about the Anglo-Saxon settlement in England is true at all; although it still survives in school teaching. I prefer to believe that Leland's results were genuine. He was president of the first European Folk-lore Congress in 1899.

Leland states that he commissioned an Italian witch, Maddalena, to collect folk-lore of all sorts. He had heard that a gospel existed and eventually she obtained a copy for him. He published this, with a translation beside it. Part of it is in verse and part in prose. Although the word gospel (*vangelo*) is perhaps too embracing a term, the work is of very great interest and forms a counterpart to Dr. Margaret Murray's researches.

The verses of the Vangelo, which appear to be of considerable antiquity, were probably handed down in oral form with little change for many centuries; but at the time they were composed, the witch cult was clearly the religion of the suppressed classes in the state, who were encouraged to murder their overlords and the Christian farmers and to blast their crops by magic. These verses were composed for a rural community, so that it is unlikely that they belong to the days of the Roman empire. It seems probable that they indicate a propaganda phase in the religion at a time when the peasant populations of western Europe had found that Church and State were both oppressors. On this ground it is likely that the Vangelo, in its present form, belongs to about the fourteenth century. 'And when the priests, or the nobility shall say to you that you should put your faith in the Father, Son and Mary, then reply: "Your God, the Father and Mary are three devils, for the true God the Father is not yours".' (Leland.)

Briefly the gospel of the witches was as follows: Tana (Diana), 'Queen of Witches All', was their goddess. Tana, the Moon, fell in love with Lucifer, the Sun, who was turned out of Paradise for his pride. As a result of this union of brother and sister, a daughter Aradia (or Herodias)[1] was born, who was the female Messiah of the witch cult. Diana, as we will call her for the present, told her daughter that, although she was a spirit, she was born only to become a mortal and to go down to earth to teach witchcraft ('stregonerie') to humanity. The witches, of whom Diana was to be the first and chief, were to be taught the secret of magic power and such arts as poisoning and crop-blasting in order that they might free the downtrodden from their oppressors.

When Aradia had finished her instruction on earth, she told her pupils that she must leave them and return to heaven. If they wished for further instruction in magic, they must ask Diana to give them the knowledge. Once a month, when the moon was full, they were to meet in some deserted spot, or in a wood, to adore Diana. They were to be naked at their meetings as a sign that they were free. They were to extinguish the lights and play the game of Benevento (apparently the game played till recently by the Eskimos, who used to put out their blubber lamps, grab the nearest woman and mate with her). After that they were to hold a sacred supper.

The ritual feast was then described. There was to be a special conjuration for each of its elements, meal, salt, honey and water. There was also a special conjuration for Cain (who was in some way related to Diana and imprisoned in the moon) to tell the fate of the suppliant in water. It is not clear, however, whether a

[1] She should perhaps be compared with the beautiful Welsh goddess Arianrod.

7

conjuration to Diana, including the baking of special cakes, is part of the same ritual, or whether it is a parallel version. This conjuration is of great interest, for in it several well-known features found in other religions can be observed: 'You shall make cakes of meal, wine, salt and honey in the shape of the crescent moon, and say: "I do not bake the bread, nor with it salt, nor do I cook the honey with the wine: I bake the body and the blood and the soul, the soul of Diana, that she know neither rest nor peace, and ever be in cruel suffering till she will grant what I request, what I do most desire, I beg it of her from my very heart! and if the grace be granted, O Diana! in honour of thee will I hold this feast and drain the goblet deep, we will dance and wildly leap, and if thou grantest the grace which I require, then when the dance is wildest, all the lamps shall be extinguished and we will freely love!" And thus shall it be done: all shall sit down to supper all naked, men and women, and the feast over, they shall dance and sing and make music, and then love in the darkness, with all lights extinguished; for it is the spirit of Diana who extinguishes them, and so will they dance and make music in her praise.' (Leland.)

After Aradia had performed her mission and Diana had recalled her, she gave her power to grant the following gifts to her devotees: success in love; to bless or curse with power; to converse with spirits; to find hidden treasure, or compel spirits of priests who had buried treasure to reveal it; to understand the voice of the wind; to change water into wine; to tell fortunes with cards, or from the hand; to cure diseases; to change ugly people into beautiful; to tame wild animals; and those who gained her favour would be granted their wishes if they importuned Aradia with the correct formula.

In Leland's gospel there follows what is evidently an alternative text. Diana, we are told, was the first act of creation. She was the first darkness and divided herself into darkness and light. The light was her other half and was her brother, Lucifer. Lucifer was so beautiful that Diana trembled with desire for him and the desire was the Dawn. Diana and Lucifer both went down to earth at its creation. Diana seduced Lucifer by assuming the form of a cat, which got into his bed and changed back into human form in the darkness. They thus became the parents of Aradia.

Diana spun the lives of men on her wheel and Lucifer turned the wheel. She turned mice into stars and became Queen of Heaven, of witches and rain.

Tana, according to Leland, was the Etruscan name for Diana. There are other traditional Tuscan stories about Diana in his book, including one telling, with witchcraft embellishments, of Diana's love for Endymion. Tana had a dog for her messenger. There are various charms in the book, but the main 'gospel' is given above and is evidently no more than a collection of fragments of myth and ritual. The underlying belief is probably of great antiquity; but, as I have said, this version does not appear to me to be older than the Middle Ages and much distorted by political propaganda.

Turning to Dr. Margaret Murray's publications, we find that, since much of her information comes from the reports of trials, from which the witches seldom escaped with their lives, the picture is somewhat different from that given by the Italian 'gospel'. There is little, if any, trace of a goddess; although modern members of the cult admit that their chief deity is female, though they may not mention her name. The evidence from the trials ranges in time from the fourteenth to the seventeenth centuries and therefore can be assumed to be more or less contemporary with the 'gospel'. Since the witches may not mention her name now, the reason why the goddess is not found in the trial accounts is presumably the same. Magic was the main purpose of Aradia's teaching and since the telling of a person's name to a magician gives him a hold over that person, it was clearly important for the witches not to mention the goddess's name to their enemies. This must be the explanation of the discrepancy.

On the other hand, there is much talk of the Devil, Beelzebub, or Lucifer, but it is quite clear that the witches regarded him as a man. To digress for a moment; it is interesting that the term 'devil' took on an evil complexion. Zoroaster (Zarathustra) was responsible for this. The various forms of 'deva', 'divus' and so on always referred to a good spirit. But Zoroaster in his teaching decided that all gods except Ahura Mazda must be some sort of demon. As they had been known as 'daevas', the term 'devil' took on an evil meaning in Persia and spread westwards with Zoroaster's cult and Mithraism. Thus it comes about that Hindu gods are Persian devils, Ahura Mazda (Ormazd), Zoroaster's

God of All Things corresponds to the Hindu Brahma and the modern conception of a Universal Mind. It is something on a different plane of thought than anything to do with Diana.

The witches' 'devil' was evidently the male leader of a coven, or group of covens; the witches being organized in groups, or squads, of twelve with a leader. There is a connection here between a 'baker's dozen' of thirteen loaves and the baking of the cakes for the ceremonial feast. The baker's dozen does not appear to have been thought unlucky in this country, but the number thirteen still is so regarded. This is due no doubt to the persecution of the witches. Dr. Murray has noted the connection between two covens and the Order of the Garter. We can all think of other examples. The use of groups of thirteen members is not confined to the witches.

The witches' devil at the trials was frequently described as appearing in the form of an animal. He was, in fact, dressed up. Although Dr. Murray produced little evidence of a belief in a goddess from the actual trials, it is clear, however, that women often took an important part in the cult. She quotes such notable instances as Joan of Arc and the Countess of Salisbury, in whose honour the Order of the Garter was instituted. The trials themselves produced ample evidence of a similar ritual to that laid down in Leland's Vangelo. With monotonous regularity the devil, the ritual feast, the dancing and the licence are described. Unlike the Vangelo, however, the devil seems to have taken the place of a kind of stud-bull in relation to all the women of his particular coven, or group of covens. For this purpose he is often described as wearing what must have been an artificial phallus. His appearance was frequently disguised as that of an ox, horse, dog, goat or other beast. Dr. Margaret Murray actually produced in her *God of the Witches* a photograph of such a disguise, the Dorset Ooser, a carved wooden mask with bulging eyes in a human face and with bared teeth. The face has bull's hair and horns. This remarkable object was stolen from the farmer who owned it. One feels that it may have returned to some hidden coven in the area. There is no hint of this dressing up in Leland's Vangelo. His ritual does not contain a mention of any priest of the cult. We have the mythical story of Diana changing into a cat in order to seduce Lucifer, but the dressing up of Dianic priests to represent animals is not even suggested in the text.

10

Of the actual beliefs of the witches standing trial in France, Germany, Great Britain, or Scandinavia there is little trace. The witches had no hesitation in admitting that they had taken part in ritual dancing, sacred feasts, sexual licence and the working of harmful magic. They never said, however, what their beliefs were, nor in whose honour their rites were performed. Dr. Margaret Murray rightly infers that the witches had little objection to being martyred for their faith and deduces from earlier material the belief in the necessity for human sacrifice of which again the Vangelo gives no hint.

It does not appear as if there was much persecution of witches before the latter part of the fourteenth century. Dr. Murray thinks that the Christian Church grew in strength until it felt it was strong enough to suppress rival cults by force. There has been little evidence from the Middle Ages that the church would not have jumped at any opportunity for doing this, but a study of the history of the times suggests an even more urgent need for the persecution. All through this time the Black Death was scourging Europe with wave after wave of devastating mortality. The number of serfs and labourers was greatly reduced everywhere. As a result, the survivors began to appreciate their greater value and importance and would no longer submit to the conditions of semi-slavery under which their fathers had laboured. In France, continually devastated by war as well as plague, there were murderous risings, Jacqueries, ruthlessly suppressed. In England matters came to a head in A.D. 1381. The Peasants' Revolt, or Wat Tyler's Rebellion as it was called in school history books, almost destroyed the whole fabric of feudal England. It was particularly directed against the Church and in eastern England was put down by a warrior bishop. The best general account of this is to be found in A. B. Steel's *Richard II*. Here we need only note that the chancellor, who was also archbishop of Canterbury, Simon of Sudbury, was seized and had his head cut off (this treasure is said to be still preserved!). The prior of Bury was dragged from his monastery and given a parody of the trial of Christ. London was at the mercy of the rebels. The crisis, however, passed in a remarkable manner. Dr. Murray has given good reasons for thinking that the Plantagenets were all devotees of the witch cult. Richard, son of the Black Prince and so descended from the founder of the Order of

11

the Garter, rode out to the rebel army and persuaded them to go home. Even when their leader was killed in a brawl by the mayor of London, they still accepted the young king as their leader. This was a most dramatic incident. London had been seized; law was at an end; the feudal overlords were utterly disorganized and unprepared; there was nothing to stop the rebels from doing exactly as they liked; and yet the young king had only to say a few words to them and they were ready to go home. The king was not representing the power of law, for the rebels had cut off the head of the chancellor; nor the Church, for they had cut off the head of its leader who was the same man. The rebels throughout the rising did in fact make the property of the Church their first target. The king, however, had complete confidence and complete authority, although he was only a boy of fourteen. It seems almost certain that he had this power, not because he was the lawful king, but because he was the accepted head of the rival religion.

If one studies the events in eastern England, where they have been worked out in some detail, it is obvious that the movement was largely anti-clerical. It was the 'learning of the clerks' which was burnt with great rejoicing in the market place at Cambridge. 'Away with the learning of the clerks. Away with it!' yelled the crowd, as they hurled the university muniments into the bonfire. There was nothing vindictive about it; although the clerks were bad landlords. It was their learning, that is their religious books, which the rioters wanted to destroy. At any rate this is how the picture presents itself to me. (I published an account of finds of weapons lost at this time in *Merlin's Island*.)

When the feudal powers recovered from their shock, and it must be remembered that many living knights had seen what devastation could be wrought by the English long bow on the finest cavalry in Europe at Crécy and Poictiers, they acted with ruthless force. The king became a boy again in the power of his councillors and his promises to the rebels were overruled. But the memory of what had happened was not forgotten by Church and State. The menace of the other religion had to be removed. Not only did it prove capable of physical force, but its devotees were all magicians and could blast man, beast and the whole process of fertility. I suggest that this was a far more powerful cause of the subsequent persecution than simple religious

12

rivalry. When, not long afterwards, for I am convinced that Dr. Murray is right in her theory, Joan of Arc united all France in arms against the English by the same power, it was clear to the rulers of the Church and State all over western Europe that the cult must be stamped out. 'Stamp it out in the name of Christianity, by all means. Yes, but we know that the real reason is political.'

If my reasoning of this question is correct, then it follows that Leland's Vangelo almost certainly dates from about this period. It is part of an infinitely older belief overlaid with political propaganda. It does not appear to be an isolated case of its kind. If scholars are correct in their deductions, the Book of Revelation is much the same kind of thing and was political propaganda cloaked in religious guise, directed at the power of Rome in the reign of Nero. From what one knows of the great tolerance shown by the Roman Empire to a multitude of wild religions, it seems most unlikely that it would have persecuted the early Christians for practising such a mild faith, unless it had seen something very dangerous in it. The Book of Revelation can be easily explained as a very violent cryptic instigation of the churches to plot in secret for the overthrow of Rome. The druids too were muzzled and largely stamped out, not because they practised human sacrifice, which was a commonplace idea in the ancient world, all that was necessary was to send out an order for it to stop; but because they were bitterly hostile to Rome and trained the young men to disregard the value of their lives. They assured them that if they died in battle they would be more quickly freed from the boredom of frequent rebirth and so reach paradise the sooner. In recently conquered lands, such a teaching was a very great danger.

We can then, I think, assume that Leland's Vangelo and Dr. Murray's trial evidence are more or less contemporary and that it is reasonable to use the two together to form a picture of the witch cult at about A.D. 1400. Stripped of tirades against oppressors, the main tenets of the religion appear to be these: The great deity who made the universe and ordered the lives of men was female. She was Diana who, to the Greek world, was known as Artemis. Diana was at first invisible, but she created light in the form of a male consort, Lucifer. He was represented by the sun, the greatest light known to men. Diana, as queen of heaven and darkness, was represented by the greatest object in the night sky, the moon. A child of the union of Light and Darkness was Magic and was known as Aradia. Aradia was sent to earth to teach this art to mankind. That is, she was, in the opinion of her devotees, a personage, known in Hindu religion as an avatar, who taught them how to harness magic power. Aradia, at some far-off time, may have been as much an historical person as Christ, Krishna, or Buddha. It is possible that her original message was not unlike theirs; but can we be sure that there was any such person?

Magic has an ugly name to those who have seen black magic at work among primitive peoples. Others think that it is completely bogus and no such power exists. But magic is simply the use of powers of the mind which are not as yet understood by science. Magic and miracle are the same thing. Telepathy is a form of magic which is becoming scientifically respectable. It was completely taboo among scientists, till certain recent experiments showed that there was something in it. Scientists did not see how it could exist, therefore it did not exist; although thousands of their fellows knew that it existed and it can be observed in use every day on the sea-shore among flocks of wading birds. Anyone who has had much to do with animals knows far more about telepathy than can be learnt by guessing games with packs of cards. But you cannot measure human observation and therefore it is not scientific. Scientists can be pretty blind from obstinacy at times.

Precisely the same story concerns the faculty of dowsing, of which water divining is a branch. This was one of the magic arts given by Aradia to her devotees. Most people can dowse, if they know how to do it. If they cannot do it, there is probably some fault in the electrical system of their bodies. But water divining was an impossibility, an absurdity; it could not concern science, even if people were using it and finding water by its means every day. Now machines are being used to do the work of the diviner's rod. Years ago, I was asked to go to Lundy Island to investigate some burials which were supposed to be Vikings. I went with a geologist, named Dollar, who had been working on the island for some time. The burials were duly located in a small grass field enclosed by stone walls and occupied by a young bull. He disapproved of our activities, tore up clods of earth with his horns and had to be slapped at intervals on his rump with the flat of a spade. Still, the burials were found and examined. They were not Vikings, for they had been buried through a layer of medieval rubbish. I have wondered whether they were some of the unfortunate prisoners who were to have been shipped across the Atlantic as slaves after the battle of Sedgemoor, but are known to have been dumped somewhere on the way. In any case, Dollar and I were left with time on our hands till the boat from Bideford called again to take us off. Amongst other activities, which included an attempt at air-photography from a kite, it was suggested that we should experiment with dowsing. We worked out fields of force round a sheet of corrugated iron lying on the ground, which were similar to those made by a bar magnet. Then, as I was rather good with the thing, Dollar proposed that I should try to locate volcanic dykes, which passed through the slate rocks at the south end of the island. These dykes, being covered with humus and grass, were invisible on top of the island. Dollar blindfolded me and, as he had no occasion to wish me ill, I walked quite happily along the path on top of the cliffs holding the twig. Every now and then the twig would turn violently in my hands for a few paces and then stop. When this had happened several times, Dollar stopped me, took off the handkerchief and said, 'You have located every one of the dykes. If I had known you could do that I should never have brought down a magnetometer from Cambridge.' Now, this was magic, but it was also a scientific experiment. Since that time I have been successful on several occasions in locating ancient ditches and graves hidden in the chalk. I am no expert in the art, but I am fully convinced that Aradia's witches when properly trained could have found their buried treasure.

Other faculties of a magical nature are slowly becoming respectable. Faith healing and healing at a distance by resonance are being widely practised. Not long ago my mother said to me, 'I don't get much rheumatism now, I go on the box'. 'What on earth is that?' I asked. 'Oh I gave a spot of my blood to a woman in Oxford and she puts me on the box and I am soon right again.' 'But this is pure magic, Ma,' I said incredulously. Since then I have read some of the literature on the subject. It is magic without a shadow of doubt, but magic conducted with an elaborate scientific apparatus. How it works, I have not the slightest idea, but it has clearly come to stay. Of course the greatest exponent of this kind of thing in all history was Christ. He had apparently very little difficulty in teaching other people to do it, and the process of teaching does not appear to have taken long. He used to get very angry with them when they lost confidence in themselves and failed to do it. There was no years of training in Yoga. It appears to have been no more than complete trust in your power to do it. If there was any further teaching necessary, it has either been lost or deliberately smothered. The power could be used for both good and evil. St. Peter's performance with Ananias and Sapphira was as perfect an example of black magic as could be found anywhere in Africa. St. Paul's confidence was evidently so great that he learnt how to heal by himself. I am not concerned here with how the power was generated, but only to show that here is perfectly good evidence for the existence of another of the faculties taught by Aradia to her devotees. Just as the Apostles could turn from white magic to black, so apparently could the witches. Once again we can see a parallel between the persecution of the early Christians by Nero and that of the witches by the Christians in the Middle Ages. Nero's government apparently took little notice of the Christians until the Jewish revolt against Rome. When, however, this broke out, with a crisis in the terrible siege of Jerusalem, which started in A.D. 67, a violent persecution of Christians ensued. Were they not famed all over the world for their magic? Were they not known to destroy their enemies by its power? Were not most of them these Jews who were busy crucifying all their prisoners on the walls of Jerusalem? If the secret police had seen a copy of the 'Revelations', the disruptive and dangerous character of the movement would have appeared obvious to them. It is a curious piece of irony that the Church, which had suffered so much from persecution itself, should have been the organization which treated the witches with even greater brutality and shows how terribly it had wandered from the teaching of its great master. It is only fair to add that it was quite as ready to burn its own members at the stake, if they happened to differ slightly from the official view in dogma.

The worship of Diana never seems to have been viewed with any disfavour in Roman times. The points which strike modern observers as being particularly unpleasing, the nudity and promiscuity at the meetings, were viewed with the detachment which is accorded to naked sadhus in India today. These sadhus insist on nudity as being essential to mental freedom in the same way as it was ordained for the witches in the Vangelo. Nudity meant little in medieval Europe. Nobody wore night clothes in bed[1] and housing conditions were so cramped that everyone must have been quite accustomed to the sight of a naked human body. The argument that nudity added to the licentiousness of the proceedings can be looked at from the opposite angle. The naked bodies of elderly witches and wizards, doubtless unwashed for a considerable time, must have exerted a depressing effect to no small degree. The answer given by modern witches to this nudity business is that clothes hamper the generation of magic power.

Power was needed for the main purpose of the meetings. This was to increase the productivity of man, beast and field by sympathetic magic. It was only later, when the religion was facing dangerous enemies, that its devotees turned to the use of black magic against them. To understand the witch cult, it is necessary to go back before the persecution, to a time when kings, great nobles and even high dignitaries of the Christian Church, not only accepted it as a matter of course, but even seem to have practised its rites.

To the summary of the Dianic beliefs which we have already made, it is necessary to add the role of the male priest. Diana was clearly represented at the meetings by a woman, or all the women present. One would have expected the priest to represent Lucifer, but instead we find him dressed up as some animal or other. There is clearly something here which does not fit into the combined picture we have already formed. By no stretch of imagination could this animal devil be thought to represent the sun. To look for him we shall have to go far back in time, before the days of churchmen burning witches at the stake and witches trying to blast the productivity of their enemies, and see what can be learnt from a brief examination of the worship of Diana in the ancient world of the Classics. Before we do this, however, there is one important point which must be stressed. It is very difficult to expect country people to believe in a great Father God without a Great Mother also. The idea

[1] Although pictures exist of bishops wearing their mitres when asleep!

makes no sense to those whose lives are bound up with the breeding of animals. Townsfolk might accept the idea, but not countrymen. Fortunately for Christianity, Pope Gregory had observed this and had provided a loophole for his priesthood. Such pagan customs as were too deep-rooted to be removed were to be turned round to look like Christian ones. For centuries therefore there was nothing strange in a man believing both in the Christian teaching and in that of Aradia.

One of the great difficulties which face anyone who attempts to unravel problems of the ancient world is that of names. A tribe may be known by one name in one century and another in the next. One author may use the name of the rulers of the tribe; another speak of it by the name used by its neighbours; a third speak of it by a kind of portmanteau geographical term. None of these need be the name by which it spoke to itself of itself. In a generation all may have changed. The rulers may now be a different clan, or family; the tribe may have migrated and be called something else by its new neighbours and its geographical setting may be completely different. It may now be known by the designation of its chief deity, or, if it has formed a new alliance, by some group name like 'the All Men' or 'the Men of the Spear'. I mentioned this difficulty when trying to study the Picts in *The Painted Men*. Now we are faced with the same trouble when dealing with gods and goddesses. The deities of antiquity have a very great number of names. Not only were they known by different names in different places, but they often had at least three different phases, old, middle-aged and young, which were all known by different names in one place. Added to this, conquerors like the Romans tended to add religions, picked up all over their empire, to such of their own gods who had some points in common. This is all terribly complicated and cannot be really disentangled in a lifetime of study. To mention two, and probably the same goddesses who come into our study, Isis is said to have had ten thousand names; the Irish Badb when questioned in a mythical tale gave thirty-one of her own. Not one of Badb's names is probably the one by which she was known in secret to her worshippers. It was like the business of not mentioning salt in an east-coast Scottish fishing-boat. You mentioned it in some roundabout way. There are traces of the former exis-

18

tence of this in Homer, when he speaks, for instance, of Zeus as the Thunderer. At one time you might not mention the name Zeus except in secret. When a Roman asked a Caledonian, through an interpreter, the name of his chief deity, he did not get the real name in reply. He got something like 'the Forest One' or 'the Long-haired One'. When he asked the name of a neighbouring tribe, the answer was 'the Newcomers' or 'the People of the Stag' or 'the Hunters'. Knowing no better, the Classical authors wrote these answers down and they have since become distorted by being turned from Celtic into Latin, from Latin into Greek and back again, with copyists' slips to make it all easier. I often wonder how near the truth are the accounts brought back by anthropologists from backward tribes. Things are made up to please them. Names may only be mentioned indirectly. Customs are invented. What sort of answer might be expected from an Irishman in Kerry to the question 'Who may marry your cousin's husband's niece?' 'Ach! that will be Micky's Pat from Ballybunion.' Neither boy nor girl happens to exist, but one must be polite to strangers and this is the kind of story that seems to please them.

In spite of these difficulties we will make some attempt at the study of Diana from the classical sources. I do not think it is my fault if the result is somewhat confusing. I will begin with the Roman version, because Leland's Tana comes from Italy and it seems sensible to make a start in that area. Diana to the Romans was the chaste huntress and on her images she carries a bow and is often accompanied by a stag. But Diana had very many different names and different attributes in the Roman world. 'Great is Artemis of the Ephesians' shouted the angry crowd as reported in the Acts of the Apostles. That was Diana's Greek name. In Egypt they would have shouted for Isis; in Palestine for Ashtoreth; in Ireland for Danu, Macha, Badb, Morrigan, or the Cailleach, or any of twenty-six other names. In Carthage her name was Tanit. Diana had many different tales told of her birth and parentage. She was frequently believed to be three persons, Diana, Proserpina and Hecate. As such she was known as Triformis. She was Cynthia, Delia, Luna, Orthia, Aricia, Agrotera, Selene, Cybele, Lucina and many more besides. Sometimes she was Proserpina and sometimes Ceres, her mother, was Proserpina. Jupiter, the Greek Zeus, was usually regarded as her father.

Diana was goddess of the moon and many surviving statue
show her with a sickle moon above her hair. Her brother w
Apollo, who was linked with the sun. Cicero tells that Apoll
came from the land of the Hyperboreans. According to Egyptia
mythology, however, Apollo was Horus and the son of Isis ar
Osiris, the moon and the sun.

As Hecate, Diana was the goddess of magic and represente
as having a woman's body with three heads. These were tl
heads of a horse, a dog and a boar. We shall hear more of th
later. Cross-roads were sacred to Hecate, who was there know
as Trivia, the goddess of the three ways. I know of no story
classical mythology which might suggest that Apollo was i
volved in a love affair with Diana. On the other hand, despi
the fact that she was the goddess of chastity, she was also tl
guardian of women in childbirth. In spite of having special pe
mission from Jupiter to remain unmarried, she had love affai
with the giant Orion, with Endymion and with the nature go
Pan. Orion and Endymion do not concern us further, but Pa
with his horned head and goat legs is another matter.

Diana, as Proserpina, was the daughter of Jupiter and Cere
Some say that Jupiter himself was so taken with her beauty th
he turned himself into a serpent and seduced her. Later she w
carried off by Pluto, god of the Underworld. At the intercessio
of her mother she was permitted to spend half the year abo
ground with Ceres and half of it with Pluto below. Proserpina
Persephone, as she was called by the Greeks, as Queen of He
was responsible for the deaths of men. Her return to the wor
above brought about the return of spring. Atropos was h
messenger and sent to snip a hair from the heads of those wl
had been marked for death. Proserpina again had many nam
such as Libitina, Core, Deois, Theogamia, Anthesphoria ar
Liberia.

Turning to the Greek world, we now have to investiga
Artemis. Artemis and Diana were thought to be one and tl
same goddess by the ancients. Yet, on the face of things, no tw
personalities could be much more different, provided they we
of the same sex. For Artemis in her Ephesian guise is a 'muck
wife'. Her statues, two of which have recently been recovere
from the site of her world-famous temple and of whi
other examples have been found as far west as Marseilles, sho

20

a matronly lady with at least three, and often more, tiers of bare breasts, superimposed like turrets on a battleship. She has an apron covered with the representations of animals. On her head she carries either the façade of a temple, or a castellated city. This is the great mother of all, the giver of fertility to man and

Fig. 1.
    (a) Sketch of wooden carving at the base of a Vancouver Island totem pole. This shows the marriage of the totem bear to a woman. Quite a number of such carvings exist. Some similar carving was probably the early form of Greek Artemis and Celtic Artio.
    (b) Artemis of Ephesus drawn from a Roman statue found in that city (after Franz Mitner). Numerous similar statues have survived.

beast and the protector of his cities. The statues show how greatly a religious conception can change through the centuries for, although these images show the type of Artemis which was venerated at the time of St. Paul, earlier Greek accounts describe the goddess as the protector of chastity (Fig. 1 (b)).
    At a still earlier time she was evidently a totem bear. It seems

21

to be reasonably clear that the chaste goddess of the Greek settlers in Asia Minor had become united with the personality of Ashtoreth, the great fertility goddess of that area, and had lost her original character in the process. She was not the great mother to the early Greeks, but became so to their descendants; shipwrecked sailors had once been sacrificed to her in ancient Greece. Now Artemis, like Isis, was the protector of shipping. She had no recorded consort at Ephesus and her priests were eunuchs, known apparently as Essenes. Though she was said by some to have been hostile to Aphrodite, the Venus of the Greeks, yet a statue of the goddess has been found in the excavations near her temple. This is all a far cry from human sacrifice to a wooden figure of a totem bear and shows how very difficult it is to form any opinion of a particular deity. The Ephesian Artemis was connected with the moon; the Artemis of Homer's day was not. The Artemis of St. Paul's day is apparently the Ashtoreth, Queen of Heaven, of the Old Testament, the Ishtar of the Carthaginians. Ishtar went down to visit the Lord of the Underworld like Proserpina of the Romans and, as Dr. Gardner records in an existing myth told by modern witches like their goddess. The Roman Proserpina therefore appears to be the Asiatic form of Artemis and Proserpina is another name for Diana.

Ishtar, Isis and Io appear to be the same goddess, who, however, was Diana in Crete and Venus in Cyprus. Like the old Greek Artemis, the Egyptian Isis had once been a totem animal before she became a Great Mother goddess. In this case the animal was a cow. Isis was greatly revered in Egypt, but some say that she was imported into Rome as Bellona. Bellona, however, was a war goddess and in Rome was the sister of Mars. Isis, however, was a mild and gentle goddess in Egypt. Artemis also at one stage had been a goddess of victory. As far as we can make anything at all of these frightful complications, it appears that this Diana-Artemis-Isis figure must have been goddess of everything, of life and death, peace and war, fertility and dearth. Men worshipped her in the particular guise which happened to appeal to them. It is easy to see why Isis was said to have had ten thousand names. We have quite enough in this chapter already. I could easily add many more to it!

The chaos and confusion which confront us when we try to understand these deities in the classical world is more apparent

22

than real. Underlying the innumerable varieties of ritual and the bewildering mass of names were only a few real beliefs. One of these was that of the great mother. She had created the universe and she ordered the lives of men from the cradle onwards. Men might call her by different names; they might worship her as a girl to obtain success in their loves; they might do so at middle age to bring success in more mundane affairs; or they might venerate her in old age to ward off death as long as possible. She represented all these things and controlled them, as she controlled sun and moon, rain and drought, wind and sky and sea. It was generally recognized that she had to have a male consort, but he was of far less moment. Only the woman could bring forth children, so only a female deity could bring forth the world. The father was incidental.

It seems probable that by far the most difficult area in which to study these old beliefs is in that eastern half of the Mediterranean where most has been recorded about them. Counter-clockwise from Egypt, through Asia Minor, round to Greece and on to Italy, invasion after invasion had taken place century after century for thousands of years. Each one had some influence on the religious beliefs of the peoples involved in it. The populations were mixed so completely that layer upon layer of belief was deposited and the degree of amalgamation of ideas varied from district to district and country to country. Some blending of ideas has taken place everywhere in the world; but nowhere to such a marked extent as in the eastern half of the ancient world. Egypt alone suffered less than other lands. The climax was reached when Rome became mistress of almost the whole of the known world. All roads led to Rome and every religion travelled along them. To try to evaluate these religions from the works of Roman writers must be as hard a task as anyone could wish; yet it is on the works of such writers that we have to lean heavily when trying to deal with matters further from the centre of disturbance.

A good example of what could happen to old cults when Rome took a hand in the matter is the case of Bellona. There was an ancient Sabine goddess named Nerio. The Romans recognized her as Duellona, who later became known as Bellona. When Sulla was in Cappadocia, the local war goddess known as Bellona appeared to him and told him to return to Rome and drench it in the blood of his enemies. He proceeded to carry out the goddess's estimable suggestion. Sulla's proscription shocked Rome by its ferocity; but, as a result of its success, the rites of the Cappadocian Bellona were instituted in Rome and added to those of the original Nerio who, ironically enough, had once been equated with Virtus.

Enough has been said to show that we are likely to become completely mesmerized if we continue to search the classical mythology for the origin of the witch cult. Each god and goddess has such a multitude of names, and such a variety of rites, that a lifetime of study would not reveal a clear-cut picture. If it did so, it would probably do no more than reflect the idea which happened to be uppermost in the mind of the man undertaking the search. We can, however, usually detect a family group of deities, a mother, father and child, to whom is often added a wicked uncle who murders the father or carries off the daughter. The heroine of the mythical story is the mother. These mythical personages and their story were clearly invented to account for the seasonal changes in nature. The seasonal changes, of course, differed from place to place and the mythical story varies with the geographical setting, at the time the story was constructed, of the tribe who invented it. The climatic conditions are reflected in the descriptions of the natures of the deities themselves. In a harsh climate the gods are naturally fiercer and less civilized than in an area where there was little appreciable seasonal variation. Where there was little seasonal change, the carrying off of a Proserpina would not occur in the myth. If this carrying-off myth should be found amongst a people living in an area of little seasonal change, it is reasonable to suppose that the story came there from an area where the change was marked. We can surely be fairly certain then that the witch cult, with its myth of the goddess going down to visit the king of the underworld, did not originate in a land like Mesopotamia or Egypt.

Another point, which comes out clearly in the classical mythology, is the frequency of myths in which both gods and goddesses change themselves into animals. The most common form of such myths consists of a goddess changing herself into an animal to avoid the amorous attentions of a god. This simple trick is always detected. The god turns himself into the appropriate male animal and succeeds in seducing the goddess. The

24

result of such a union was invariably fertile. This form of myth is something to do with totemism, but few scholars are agreed on what totemism is. Totemism is some mystic relationship between a group of men and a particular species of animal or even plant. But the exact relationship has defied scholarly definition. And well it might do so. It seems to be a kind of hangover from much earlier times, when men are thought to have really believed that they were physically related to animals. I find this a bit difficult to believe, for how could a man have regarded a lobster as a blood relation, unless he had already read Darwin's *Origin of Species*? Totemism was an indefinable magico-religious idea and the totem animal was in a sense worshipped. It could give help to men belonging to its own particular brand and they must not kill it without permission. Why they should have thought that it would ever willingly give such permission is another puzzle. Many scholars have noted evidence for totemic beliefs in the Upper Palaeolithic period of at least 12,000 years ago and the Rev. A. C. Armstrong, in his *Folk-lore of Birds*, has recently drawn attention to this again.

This totem concept was very strong and widespread. It probably went at one time to every corner of the inhabited world. When we find ancient European tribes called Chatti, or Epidii, we can be reasonably certain that their totem animals were once cats or horses respectively. It is also highly probable that many of the animals which appeared as heraldic blazons on the shields of medieval knights were once the totems of the families which bore these on their arms. I hope to show later on that this is not a fantastic suggestion; neither is it disregarded by some of the experts of the College of Heralds.

As civilization slowly developed and spread over wider areas, totemism began to be replaced by beliefs of a different kind. Gods and goddesses came to be imagined in human form. In this anthropomorphism man conceived gods to be made in his image and not vice versa. Forces of nature and celestial bodies were gods and they were like men. The changing of a god, or goddess, into an animal seems to me to be a symbolic way of saying, 'Our tribal deity is really a god, or a goddess, produced by the union of the animal which is our totem with the great mother, or great father', as the case may be. I do not think it necessary to assume, as does Robert Graves in his *Greek Myths*, that there was necessarily a human marriage of the priestesses of some local cult with the men of an invading tribe. All that was necessary was to explain to simple people why their totem animal was being replaced by something less easily seen, but more human. It was a change which was not always completely carried out. Pan always retained his horns and goat legs. Demeter with her horse's head is another; while Hecate with her three different animals' heads clearly represents the amalgamation of three different totems, each with its separate beast. Sometimes the totem animal evidently did not attain the status of a deity. Centaurs and satyrs are examples of this type of mythical creation. Most mermaids belong to the group, but Artemis in one phase had the form of a mermaid, half woman and half fish.

The changing of totem into deity was found all over the old world; in India, Egypt, Assyria, Greece, Italy and the Celtic lands. The marriage of the totem animal to human being is even found in the mythology and art of the North American Indians (Fig. 1 (a)). Since myths appear to be the oral counterparts of religious rites, we must surely assume that wherever we find a myth of this shape-changing kind, then there was once a religious performance in which men, or women, dressed up in the skins of the former totem animal and went through the performance which the myth describes. Here then is the clue to why the devil of the witches, the priest of the coven, appeared so frequently in animal guise. He represented the totem animal marrying the Great Mother. Since such marriages were always fertile, fertility for the tribe must naturally result.

This surely brings us a little nearer to the reason why such curious rites survived for so long a time. They were once the universally accepted method by which general productivity had to be obtained. The priest simply had to be a 'stud-bull', otherwise if crops failed, or if cattle miscarried, he would be blamed for not performing the needful magic. In the same way, kings, who bore the same responsibility over a large area, had, as Sir James Fraser and Dr. Margaret Murray have amply demonstrated, to be destroyed after a period of years, before their power of productivity, invested in them by the gods, began to wane, and the prosperity of the people as a whole suffer with it.

The witch cult then seems to me to have originated at a time when the belief in totemism was on the wane and was being superseded by a belief in gods of human form. When it was begun it was still necessary to explain to the people in general the relationship between the two beliefs in a ritual performance. Since it is generally the male priest who is dressed up, it is surely the Great Mother who represents the new idea. She is taking the place of the old totem animal and is the more important figure. Since it is the kings who are killed and not their consorts, the same conditions hold good. Had a male god been of greater importance, such conditions would have been unnecessary. It was the Great Mother who needed a frequent renewal of virile consorts. A Father God would have required a succession of wives. We can then, I feel, be reasonably certain that the cult came into being when the female principle was recognized as being the most important thing in tribal belief. That is, males had not yet asserted their right to order the doings of the tribe, or their right to succeed to the rulership of it. The organization was matriarchal and matrilineal. Such an organization had already vanished from Homeric Greece about a thousand years before the birth of Christ. But there is ample evidence from the Greek myths that it had once existed there. Two thousand years later there were still traces of the mother's greater importance in parts of Scotland and Ireland.

According to Dr. Gardner, modern witches believe in reincarnation. Their prayers are directed to the Lord of the Underworld, who is responsible for arranging where and when they shall be born again. They naturally wish to be born again in a group which will contain those persons whom they loved in this existence. According to their mythology, their great goddess went down to see this Lord of the Underworld and they eventually became lovers. The Queen of Heaven and All Living Things was mated to the Lord of the Dead and so could presumably influence him as to the reincarnation of her devotee. This is the story of Pluto and Proserpina, but with a difference. There is no reference in the classical story to the reincarnation of Proserpina's devotees and we have no means of telling whether reincarnation was ever part of their faith.

Reincarnation is a very ancient faith. Numerous scholars have seen indications of it in the burial customs of the Upper Palaeolithic period in Europe. The male skeleton found in Pavisland

Cave, on the Gower peninsula, known as the Red Lady of Pavisland, had been reddened with ochre. This is thought to indicate that he was expected to be born again of a ruddy hue, or at least in his war paint. After centuries of repression, the belief in reincarnation is beginning to be held once more today. It was a widely-held belief of the early Christians, which was declared to be a heresy in the sixth century. Caesar tells us that the Druids of Gaul believed in reincarnation of the type known as transmigration. This includes the possibility of a person being reborn in animal form. Scholars over the centuries have been puzzled how a belief which they thought had been invented by Pythagoras could have reached western Europe before the Roman conquest. This was not the only belief which caused surprise. Tacitus was unable to understand how it came about that peoples living round the Baltic should be worshipping Isis.

In the same way, modern scholars are surprised at finding many beliefs among the North American Indians which were widely held in the old world. There was, in fact, never any great obstruction to the spread of ideas around the world once man had learnt to build a boat. There is no long sea passage from Asia to North America and at one time it was shorter than it is today. On his feet, or with a boat, man could go anywhere. With a horse and a sail he could go faster. Where a man went, his ideas went too. It is as simple as that. You do not need a mass migration to carry an idea, whether it is the shape of a tool, or a belief in a god. A single man can carry it. Whether he will be believed is another matter and often depends on vested interests among his hearers. If such a man, with a higher religious concept, arrives in a tribe where there is no established priesthood and which practises nothing but some simple form of magic, he will have a good chance of implanting his belief on that tribe. In the course of generations too, he stands a good chance of being remembered as a god; particularly if his cultural level in other ways is higher than that of his hosts. If, however, he comes to a tribe where there are witch doctors, or priests, with their food to win, he is just as likely to find himself in the stockpot unless he is very 'quick on the draw'. Some worshippers of Artemis promptly sacrificed to the goddess all shipwrecked sailors who fell into their hands. No doubt her priestly officials saw to it that no doubtful beliefs should reach their congregation and interfere with their revenue.

Whether brought by merchants, or immigrants, the belief in reincarnation, or rather transmigration, had reached north-western Europe two thousand years ago and probably long before that. If we may believe the traditions recorded in the Triads of the Welsh Barddas, the belief reached Britain in the fifth century before Christ, less than a hundred years after the time of Pythagoras. The immigration of the Cwmry, described in the Triads as arriving in eastern England about 450 B.C., corresponds in a remarkable way with the immigration of the earliest iron-using peoples into that part of the country. This has only been made clear by archaeological research during this present generation. The Triads were published in 1862, long before such research was thought of. This is a strong point in favour of the tradition being genuine, despite the criticism of Victorian scholars. The internal evidence of the Triads themselves makes it very improbable that they could be anything but genuine. There are, for instance, several versions of the Triads in one manuscript, each with a different amount of interpolation from Christian teaching. The connection between the Bardic, that is Druidic, beliefs and the Hindu Upanishads is obvious. Several of the documents are stated to have been copied from a collection which was destroyed with the originals by Roundhead soldiery in the Great Civil War. This makes the comparatively recent copying of Indian beliefs most improbable, even if anyone had thought it worth his trouble to do so. There are bogus parts of the collection known as Barddas, but the Triads are not these parts. We may, I think, accept them as being genuine Welsh tradition of very great age.

In the Triads there is not the slightest trace of anything connected with the worship of Diana. They are on an entirely different plane of thought and show a belief in the progress of the soul from life to life, down into the Abyss and up again, which is surprisingly like many modern conceptions. Stripped of their Welsh terms they might have come from a book by Aldous Huxley. If then these Triads are a true reflection of Druidic belief, brought in by the first Welsh-speaking colonists of Britain, the Diana worship of the witches comes from an entirely different source. The belief in reincarnation may be a later addition to it, derived from Druidism, or some other cult. The Dianic religion represented a stage in the transition from totemism to anthropomorphism. The religion of the witches was mainly this, but now includes a belief in reincarnation, which may have been contemporary or may have come from some other cult.

I have mentioned the great difficulty experienced in trying to disentangle the beliefs of the classical world, where so much mixing of populations has occurred. It seems that it ought to be easier to make the attempt farther from this confused centre. Religions and ideas spread like ripples. The Middle East is like the middle of a pond, into which boys throw stones one after the other. The stones seldom land in the same spot. In the middle all is muddled water. Farther out, however, there are clear rings of ripples. They run through each other, but it is perfectly easy to watch any particular series of rings. It ought to be the same with these rings of thought. Some will be bigger than others and run farther across the world. Some will reach isolated corners and stay there. Out near the limits of their spread, far from the place where the stones of ideas were thrown in, it should be possible to see the ripples individually. At any rate, there is no harm in trying to do so.

Here is an example. A few years ago, during the excavations at prehistoric Jericho, a heap of human skulls was found. They had been plastered over with clay, which was moulded carefully to represent a human face, and cowrie shells had been set in the eye-sockets with the slits outwards to represent eyes. Within the present century, precisely the same treatment was given to human skulls by the head-hunting tribes of New Guinea. There they were often placed at the foot of a rude wooden figure, or suspended from one. It seems most improbable that these two examples of treating a skull in this way were independent inventions. There is, in fact, considerable evidence for head-hunting far back in the Palaeolithic period. We must surely assume that the rite in New Guinea was a survival of a custom once practised in ancient Jericho. The head-hunters too were in much the same stage of cultural development; yet their physical type appears to have been very different. It seems clear then that we are not dealing with a racial migration to distant lands, where the people remained and continued in their traditional ways for some four thousand years, but with a diffusion of ideas, ripples of thought, which spread to a limit and there stuck till such time as they could be replaced by something of a higher nature.

The former head-hunters have now undertaken a remarkable experiment in evolution. As a result of prolonged contact with peoples of more developed culture during the Hitler war, they have deliberately adopted a modern way of life at one bound, instead of advancing step by step. They have moved their villages, to break traditional ties; adopted a system of representative councils; put on western clothes and cut their mops of fuzzy hair. Magic and head-hunting are replaced by wireless and wrist-watches. The idea of such a change was apparently entirely their own. They have been caught in a fresh wave of ideas and accepted them without regret or sentiment for their former adherence to the ways of prehistoric Jericho. Such a change was far more drastic than that carried out by the Japanese at the end of the nineteenth century and probably the most remarkable experiment ever conducted by a group of men.

After this digression we can return to our main problem. We will try to pick up the threads of the inquiry near the edges of the old world and not at its heart; but we will use any information which seems to be helpful from the central area.

The Celts were spread in a great curve, from Spain in the west to Galatia in Asia Minor in the east, at the back of the Mediterranean civilizations. The Greeks called these peoples Keltoi; the Romans called them Gauls. How far they were a homogeneous people, nobody can say. Theories based on archaeological discoveries in central Europe probably explain the immediate origins of Celtic tribes at a late stage in their development, but hardly seem adequate to account for their numbers when once they began to move across the ancient world. The origin of the Celts is intimately bound up with the origin of the great family of peoples known variously as the Aryans, or the Indo-Europeans. The language and customs of the Aryan conquerors of India and the Celts in western Europe do not appear to have differed to any marked extent. Their religious beliefs were apparently much the same also. Where and when all this came from is still something which is in the guessing stage. We have to picture something a very long

31

time ago; some area where there was a highly intelligent group of men, who worked out systems of society, land tenure, farming and religious belief of a freer and more imaginative kind than anything produced in the huddled primitive cities of the east. Their haunting pipe tunes, which still thrill us today, coming across the waters of some quiet loch in the evening, went to India as well as to the Western Ocean's coasts. Their love of horses will never die as long as there are horses for them to enjoy. It is not surprising then to learn from Roman sources that they worshipped the Celtic Artemis, whose rule covered the whole animal world and to whom the hunter must make his offering before he killed any beast. Although the native name for Artemis is not given in classical accounts, yet inscriptions to a bear goddess 'Artio' have been found in Roman Gaul, which remind one of the primitive totem form of Artemis in Greece. The famous horse goddess, Epona, is more closely related to our search, for she represents the phase of religious development which we find in the witch cult. The worship of Epona spread to Rome with the cavalry regiments which were recruited in Gaul. According to the myth preserved there, Epona, whose Gaulish name is related to the Roman *equus* and Greek *'ippos*, was the child of a father in human shape by a mare. She thus bears a close relationship to horse-headed Demeter and Hecate. It seems reasonable to think that both Epona and Artio were names for the Celtic Artemis. In Roman symbolism Epona often carries a key in her hand, which is thought by some scholars to be the key of the stables. I find this explanation too trivial. Epona was a great goddess and not a mere healer of spavin or splint. The key surely represents the power to unlock the doors of life and heaven. On other occasions, when her representations carry a whip, this can hardly be so small a matter as an indication of her desire for speed. It is more likely that it shows her preparedness to chastise wrongdoers. Had an account of the ritual connected with Epona survived, it is probable that it would have explained much that we want to know and given us the key to stories which are only found today in the Irish writings of a later time, or in recorded scraps of folk-lore. We will return to Epona later on (Fig. 2 (a)).

Since most of the Gaulish gods and goddesses are known only from inscriptions on monuments, or brief accounts by Roman

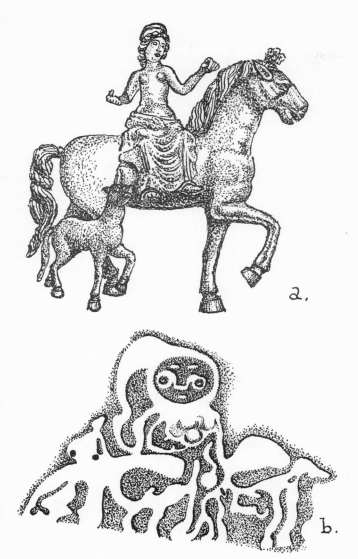

2.

b.

Fig. 2.

    (a) Sketch of Gallo-Roman bronze of Epona with her mare (Mother?) and foal. The mare is of 'forest' type and was probably therefore a grey.

    (b) Plan of Magog as excavated at Wandlebury. The goddess is 77 ft. high, her stallion 105 ft. long. Note Magog's four breasts, cut in the chalk rock.

writers, it is a matter of great difficulty to deduce much about them. One thing, however, is very clear. Early Iron Age Celtic art is full of representations of a horned deity. The drawing of the horns is sometimes mistaken for foliage by scholars, but they are horns none the less. The representations are of bull's, ram's and stag's antlers on a male head, the bull's horns often appearing like lobes above the forehead. This is clearly a nature god of the type of Diana's lover, Pan. In one fortunate case the name of this deity is preserved on a stone carving found in Paris. He was Cernunnus, or Cernunnos. There is one remarkable thing about Cernunnus: not only does he wear an open neck-ring, or torque, like many Celtic men and some women, but he sometimes holds this torque in his hand or wears it on his antlers (Fig. 3 (a)). He introduces us to a third religious phase which, in eestern Europe, does not appear to have been completely accepted in England before A.D. 100 and in Scotland before A.D. 1000. This change was of a revolutionary character, for it led to the supremacy of the male line of descent and male rule over the former descent through the female and kingship obtained through marriage with the female heir. With this change in human affairs, the male god became of greater importance than the female consort. Cernunnus by holding the torque in his hand shows that he had adopted this lunar symbol, which by right belongs to Artemis. When he is also found on sculpture associated with Apollo, Diana's brother, the picture becomes clearer. Cernunnus has taken the place, in Gaul at any rate, of the Celtic Artemis, who may be assumed to have been his consort. The steps in this deduction may seem weak, but there is more to the argument than this.

Diana was associated with the moon. She was frequently shown on Roman sculpture with a stag beside her. She was the goddess of every kind of beast, but in particular of those which showed her symbol of a sickle moon on some part of their body. The horns of oxen and sheep, the antlers of deer, the hooves of horses and the tushes of boars all fulfilled this condition. Furthermore, as we shall see later, the high stems and sterns and the curved hulls of ancient ships fulfilled the same condition. Pan, the great nature god, was Diana's lover: Apollo, associated with the sun, was her brother. Apollo came from the land of the Hyperboreans, the land behind the north wind. Diana changed

34

into a cat to avoid Typhon as a serpent. Cernunnus was evidently the great nature god of the Celts, the equivalent of Pan, but he has the moon's torque. He is sometimes shown holding a serpent in his hand. He is found associated with Apollo. He, the northern form of Pan, has usurped the attributes of his consort.

In fact, at the time the Romans conquered Gaul, the change from Mother rule to Father rule had already taken place among the ruling classes. Nothing to suggest that it had not done so is found in classical literature; but it is found in accounts of events which happened in Britain a century later.

The witch cult, however, with its great emphasis on the supremacy of the goddess, clearly developed at a time when this change, the reversal of the roles of Mother and Father, had not yet taken place in the land of its birth. Since it was widespread in Gaul in the Middle Ages, it must surely have been a submerged belief at the time of the Roman Conquest and boiled up again later on.

Pan, however, was not Diana's only consort. According to the witches' Gospel, Lucifer, the sun, was her lover and the father of Aradia. In Gaul Belenus was the equivalent of Apollo and Belenus was another name, or form, of Ogmius. Ogmius was the Celtic Hercules and the god of speech and writing: although Hercules was not the official sun god in classical Rome, yet Belenus was the sun god to the Gauls. When Hiram, king of Tyre, set up the image of Baal in a temple which was famous in the ancient world, Baal

Fig. 3.

(a) Sketch of a god with inscription 'Cernunnos' found beneath Notre Dame Cathedral.

(b) Sketch of a copy by L'Abbé Breuil of a palaeolithic man from a cave in Ari ge, wearing a stag mask, warpaint and a pony's tail.

35

was depicted as Hercules with his club. This was somewhere near the same time as Homer, about the beginning of the first millennium before the birth of Christ. It has been suggested that Baal was once a female deity, but by this time he was certainly male. The Celtic Belenus and the Phoenician Baal appear to have been identical, although one is found at the eastern end of the Mediterranean and the other in western Europe. Furthermore, it seems reasonable to say that Lucifer, the light-bearer, is Baal. We may be wrong in this, but everything in this line of research is a matter of inference. You might say that atoms do not exist, because they cannot be seen. Yet they can be inferred and split as everybody knows, sometimes to their great disadvantage. The inference then is that Lucifer, Belenus, Baal, Hercules and Ogmius are all names for the sun god and lover of Diana, Artemis, Isis or Bellona, the moon and earth goddess. Pan, or Cernunnus, the nature god, was also her lover, although he had horns and hooves. In fact, wherever we turn, we seem to come upon traces of a single underlying belief in which the male and female principles of nature are worshipped as gods and goddesses in human form. They may have a mass of different names and varying attributes, but they all represent phases of the same two deities, or powers. As we follow this ripple even farther out from its unknown source, we will find these two principles known by the homely names of Ma and Dad. The worship of whatever forces were believed to be the origin of new life appears to have been the earliest and most persistent of religious ideas.

Chapter Three

WHEN Professor W. J. Sollas wrote his *Ancient Hunters* in 1911, he was able to point to an affinity between the Upper Palaeolithic hunters of western Europe and the Eskimo of the early twentieth century. He could show a close resemblance between many objects used by the Eskimo and those of Palaeolithic man. More than that, he could compare the shapes of skulls of modern Eskimos with that of a Palaeolithic skull found at a place called Chancelade and show that they were very much alike. I once asked my friend the late W. H. L. Duckworth, who had a European reputation for knowledge of these matters, whether he thought the Chancelade skull was that of an ancient Eskimo. He replied that, if it were put amongst a collection of modern Eskimo skulls, he would not be able to tell the difference.

Duckworth was so cautious in his statements that this was good enough for me. There were clearly people living in the French caves in those early days who were indistinguishable from modern Eskimos in their bony structure. But recent archaeological work in Arctic Canada and Alaska appears to show that the earliest Eskimos in America had a very different collection of tools and ornaments from those compared by Sollas to those of Upper Palaeolithic man. Some of the earliest indeed seem to have been acquainted with the use of iron and with the art of China, or perhaps Indonesia. Their objects are so elaborate in form and decoration and their way of life apparently so different, that the only resemblance one can see to Upper Palaeolithic man is in their extremely finely made flint implements.

Their homes were square log houses with a central fire and give one the impression of having been those of a people who had once lived in a warmer climate and were adapting themselves to Arctic conditions. More recently, however, remains of yet earlier Eskimos have been found in caves in Alaska, which

37

suggests that the evolution of recent Eskimo culture may not have been derived by way of the elaborate equipment I have mentioned and Sollas may yet be right. There were perhaps many tribes of Eskimo who migrated from Asia into America. Some had been for a time in contact with more advanced civilizations, others had not. Some invented new methods of hunting whales and other sea beasts; while some, like the Caribou Eskimo of the Barrens of northern Canada, remained in a state scarcely to be distinguished from that of Palaeolithic man. All, however, appear to have kept the characteristic Eskimo type of skull, which rises like a penthouse to a ridge on the top. It is not fanciful therefore to note comparisons between the folk-lore of Eskimos and things we can infer from archaeological research done on the contents of the Palaeolithic caves in Europe. Few things are so hard to destroy as superstitions. Not many men willingly infringe an ancient taboo, even if they have only heard it for the first time a few days before on a wireless broadcast from the B.B.C.

Palaeolithic cave art has fascinated people almost more than any other archaeological discovery. That primitive hunters of bison and reindeer, at a time when even the use of metal had not been thought of, should have been able to depict with such skill the animals on which they fed, amazes the man of today. And well it might, for his greatest accomplishments in this direction seem to be confined to things made with pipe-cleaners and bits of wire, or stones with holes bored in them. The civilized man of today, however, does not spend much of his life lying behind a boulder on a bare hillside to watch every movement of a herd of deer, in the hope that he will be able to get close enough to one of them to kill it and so quiet the gnawing pains of hunger in his empty belly. It would be more surprising to me if Palaeolithic man, provided that he could draw at all, and many simple people can draw extremely well, should have drawn his animals badly. Every curve of their bodies, and every movement that they made, must have been stamped into his mind like 'Calais' on Queen Mary's heart. It is social man, and particularly urban man, who begins to produce the abortions which pass for modern art and reflect the chaos of his soul. What Palaeolithic man could not see, because they were hidden in grass or heather, were the feet of his animals. These he drew from dead beasts

38

flung down after they had been carried back to his cave. Many of his drawings were, in fact, made from dead beasts. You have only to turn pictures of the bison from Altamira upside-down to see that they were stiff from rigor mortis when they were drawn and had been carried home slung from a pole. This point was noted long ago, but has been studiously disregarded by scholars who rhapsodize on the vigour of the ancient art. However I have seen so many dead beasts carried in, stags, bears and so on, that I have no doubt at all about it. Nor has a single person with similar experience to whom I have mentioned it doubted the fact. The only reason why I have digressed on this point is because the big paintings in the caves were clearly done for a magical purpose. The hunters wanted the beasts dead and not scampering off laughing at them. When they wanted a dead beast, they drew a dead beast. When they wanted to amuse themselves, they carved or drew live beasts from memory.

The main object of painting animals on the walls of caves was sympathetic magic. If you made a good enough picture of the animal you wanted to eat, then by magic you would obtain the food you wished for. You had, however, to perform the correct ritual and I should be surprised if blood, or fat, of the kind of animal in question was not mixed with the paint used to portray it.

We are not, however, making a study of hunting magic; but searching for the origins of a religion. Deep in the recesses of caves, far beyond the reach of daylight, the hunters conjured up beasts for the pot by the flickering light of tiny blubber lamps; but they also painted monstrous human figures, which are usually known as 'sorcerers' by students of the subject. The most celebrated of these sorcerers in the Trois Frères cavern is clearly meant to represent a man dressed in the mask of a reindeer, with its antlers upon his forehead (Fig. 3 (b)). His little eyes still peer out at you from inside his disguise. This figure may be interpreted in at least two ways. It may be taken as a magician dressed to take part in some ceremony designed to produce food for the tribe; or it may show a hunter disguised for the purpose of stalking deer. It is possible that totemistic beliefs grew out of this hunting device. Hunters observing the instant alarm which affected their quarry when it saw or smelt a man, and its relative disregard for the near approach of one of its own kind, must have thought out the idea of disguising themselves in a skin which both looked and smelt correctly. From this thought may have developed something like this: 'When I dress up in the skin of a stag, I take on the appearance of a stag. When I take on the appearance of a stag, I can approach other stags as if I were one of themselves. For the time being I am as if I were a stag. The stag's skin belongs to me and is part of me, and yet it is still the skin of a stag. It has qualities which the other stags recognize as their own. When wearing my stag's skin, I am as it were a stag. I must then be related to the stag in some way.' Nobody knows how the totem idea arose. This is simply a possible suggestion of the way in which, by frequent use of such a disguise, hunters may have come to think of themselves as in some way related to the beasts they hunted. In their magic in the dark gloom of the caves, they may not only have tried to entice the quarry into their power, but asked its permission to kill it because it was one of them. They also probably performed other ritual to ensure that there would be a plentiful supply of the animals in question. There would presumably have been at least three ceremonies to be performed: (1) to ask permission from the stags to kill one of their number; (2) to endow the hunters with the qualities of the skin; (3) to ensure that the numbers of the stags did not diminish, but increased. For (2) the hunter had to be temporarily turned into a stag-man. For (3) it seems most probable that he would have to go through the act of procreation with a woman dressed in the skin of a hind. Although there is no real evidence of this, there is at least a slender clue. A well-known carving from a French cavern shows a gravid female figure, half deer and half woman. This at least shows that there was some idea of relationship between the two species in the mind of the man who made the carving. We are following very slender clues. The remarkable thing is not that the clues are slender, but that, after the passage of perhaps 12,000 years, there are any clues to follow at all. There are enough of them, however, for the Rev. E. A. Armstrong in his recent *Folk-lore of Birds* to be able to suggest that various ideas noted in the cave art travelled all round the world and survived in places till the present day.

I think we must take notice of every clue and, instead of complaining how few they are, meditate for a moment on how many prayer books you would be likely to find in the midden of a

Highland shooting-lodge. Assuming that the clues are of importance, let us see what they may be thought to indicate. First they tell us that belief in the potency of magic was widely believed at a time when herds of reindeer were common in France and great carapaces of ice spread far out over the foothills of the Alps. Secondly, they show that this magic was apparently aimed at securing an abundance of food. Thirdly, they suggest that the germ of totemism was already there and that marriage with the totem animal to ensure its productivity had probably been enacted as a sympathetic magical ritual by humans dressed in the skins of the totem beasts. Here, surely, is the embryo of an ancestral witch cult. I think we can go even further than this. If women went into the deep recesses of the caves, where they were probably forbidden to go at other times, for a symbolic marriage ceremony, is not this the origin of the myth of Pluto and Proserpina and the one preserved among the witches of today? The chief magician, the shaman, angakok, the father of the tribe, or whatever he was, is already well on the road to becoming a horned god, a Cernunnus, or Pan.

Dr. Margaret Murray arrived at much the same conclusion in her *God of the Witches*. When her next book appears, I have no doubt it will tell us a great deal more and all I have written on this subject will appear very superficial. Nevertheless I hope that by the time this book comes to an end there may be a few suggestions in it that my old friend has not thought of.

In the Upper Palaeolithic then, if we may trust the inferences I have made from our slender clues, there was an idea in existence which might blossom out into a full-fledged religion. At present, however, it is without its chief deity. There is no Diana. This is not surprising. In a population which lives exclusively by hunting, the hunter is far more important than his squaw. She may cut up and cook the meat; scrape the fat off the skins and peg them out to dry; chew them till they are soft enough to use; cut up the rawhide thongs; bring in the firewood; collect roots and nuts; bear the new generation of hunters and do all the less attractive work of the community. But the man goes out and gets the meat at risk of life and limb. On him the life of everyone depends. When he has brought in the game, he can lie about and whittle bones, flake arrowheads out of flint, or just sit in the sun whistling to himself. He is the boss. No Great Mother idea is likely to be born in such a setting, or if it does come, the Great Mother will only be a consort and squaw to the Great Father. There are no monstrous female figures painted on the cave walls. There may be numerous little ivory carvings of gross or slender women and even a frieze of women's legs showing anatomical details at the top. But this kind of thing need not have any greater significance than a general interest in sex. There is one carving of a woman holding out a horn, which in a later period would certainly be taken for a goddess offering a horn of plenty. Perhaps this is what it does suggest; although we have as yet no hint that an idea of anthropomorphic deities had arisen in the minds of men. The Eskimos, like some other Mongolian peoples, had no real religion. They had shamans, who could talk to spirits of various kinds; but there were no deities. Palaeolithic man probably resembled them in this. Some of the statuettes undoubtedly represent pregnant women and may therefore correspond to the little ivory talismans found in old Eskimo ruins. It was desirable to have children in a world where accidental death was presumably common and the expectation of life short. Few Eskimo hunters used to live beyond the age of forty-five. By that time they became too slow in their reactions to cope with the dangers of their calling. The sea, or the walrus, or the bear claimed them. I have seen a kayak paddle, thrown up by the sea, on the shore of a deserted island off the coast of Greenland, which was probably the only remaining piece of evidence of such a tragedy. It would have been much the same for Palaeolithic man. The rush of a bison would be just as hard to avoid as that of a walrus. So children were needed if the tribe was to survive. People who used magic to obtain their food, doubtless employed it also to get their children. There is, however, nothing to show that a Great Mother was importuned to that end. Perhaps it is more probable that the fertility of their women was regarded as good magic in itself. The young Eskimo hunter, when he had killed his first seal, had to handle a girl in an intimate fashion. It is remarkable also that the frankly amoral game of 'Lights Out', or Benevento, was played by both Eskimos and witches.

We seem to be looking at a phase in history in which part of an ancestral witch cult had developed, but the essential goddess of the full religion had not yet made her appearance.

Furthermore, although Dr. Murray has drawn attention to

the well-known painting at Cogul in Spain in which a ring of dancers is apparently shown, the dancers are not naked, or of mixed sexes, but clothed and all women. They are dancing round the phallic figure of a man. If this painting represents a ritual dance for the production of fertility magic, it is directed towards the male and not the female principle.

With the disappearance of the Palaeolithic hunters and their art from north-west Europe, we are left without clues in that area for thousands of years. I can see nothing in the archaeology there to help us. Some remarkable antlered heads were found in an excavation of the site of a hunter's camp at Star Carr in Yorkshire by Professor J. G. D. Clark. These are pieces of the frontal bones from skulls of red deer with the antlers still attached. The bones are roughly detached from the skulls and holes have been cut carelessly in order to fasten the bones and antlers to something. Neither the edges of the slabs of bone nor the edges of the holes have been smoothed off. The antlers themselves, like many detached specimens found on the site, have been much reduced in size and considerably mutilated by the removal of strips of horn with a flint burin. The strips of horn were then utilized to make barbed points, often wrongly spoken of as harpoons, for tipping fish-spears, or other implements. It has been suggested that these antlered 'heads' were used either in ritual dances or as disguises for hunters. These ideas do not seem probable. No one would willingly use a mutilated object, and one moreover which would chafe holes in his skin, for a ritual dance. The supernatural powers would undoubtedly be offended at such casual behaviour. Nor would a hunter use a disguise of this character when the whole point of it was to look as like the living beast as possible. The gashes made by the burin on the antlers would show up as glaring white streaks for a long distance. I think the real purpose of these objects was of a far simpler nature. Considerable force was needed to cut grooves in the antlers for detaching the strips of horn. One hand had to hold the antler, while the other used the burin. If, however, you strapped the detached slab of bone with the antlers on it to an upright post or tree-trunk, you could use both hands to work the burin and bring more force behind its stroke. The rest of the skull went into the family stew before the brains rotted inside it. So, interesting as these objects are, I fear they are of no value to our present investigation.

43

Chapter Four

WE learnt from the witch trials that a horned male figure once played an important part in the witch ritual and there appears to be good reason for thinking that this figure originated far back in Palaeolithic times. In classical story, the horned god Pan, the nature god, was one of Diana's lovers. In Gaulish art a horned figure is often worked into their intricate ornamental patterns (Fig. 4(b)) and it is reasonable to think that this is a Celtic Pan. Under the influence of classical art the Gauls produced sculptures of some of their gods and one of these, antlered and wearing a torque, is known to be named Cernunnus (Fig. 3(a)). In one group he sits, holding a horn of plenty, crowned with stag's antlers, with Apollo and Mercury. Caesar reported that Mercury was the greatest of the Gaulish gods, but it is clear that the Mercury of the Gauls bore little resemblance to the Mercury of Rome. One of his Gaulish names was certainly Esus, which is apparently a variation of the Greek Zeus; but he seems also to have been represented in triple form as Ogmius, Teutates and Taranis. Ogmius was a Hercules complete with club. It seems then that Cernunnus is a more direct ancestor of Diana's lover, Pan, than is the Palaeolithic shaman in the depths of the caves. In modern witch ritual I can find no mention of any male deity, except a Lord of the Underworld, who may be this same cave 'sorcerer' (Fig. 3(b)).

The modern witches have a myth, in which he is visited by the Queen of Heaven, who becomes his mistress. This story seems to be a variant of the classical myth of Pluto and Proserpina, but it is so widespread that there is no reason for supposing that it came from the Romans, or from the Greeks. We will leave this problem for the moment, with the thought in our minds that the

44

Lord of the Underworld may well have been the same Palaeolithic sorcerer whose picture figures in the French caves and
was there perhaps 10,000 years ago.

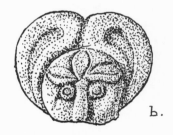

Fig. 4.
    (a) Sketch of the 'Devil's Stone', Copgrove, near Ripon.
        A left-handed, horned figure, very worn and indis-
        tinct. Perhaps first century A.D. (after Major).
    (b) Horned stone, Celtic head from Heidelberg (after
        Jacobsthal). Note 'third eye' (see Fig. 7).

Diana's lover in the witches' Vangelo was not Pan, but Lucifer. Lucifer the light-bearer figures in the witch trials and is
alternatively known as Beelzebub, or the Devil. Lucifer was
known over much of Gaul, Britain and Ireland as Lugh (the
Latin: Lux). Places like Lyons in France still bear his name, for

Lyons was once Lugudunum, Lugh's dun, or fort. Lugh's name still survives in Britain today. There is a Lugmoor on the hill just above the house where I am writing this. There is also a Bulstone, which is Bel's stone and Bel is Beelzebub. In fact the place is dotted with names derived from the worship of the old gods. On the opposite side of the combe is Elverway. Elva was Lugh's sister-in-law. The combe itself is Branscombe (Cwm Bran) and Bran is Lugh in the form of a raven. The ravens still nest on the cliff and give me great pleasure when they fly over croaking, for the raven's croak is always thought to be lucky by the Gael, and ravens are most attractive birds.

Probably this kind of thing can still be found all over the west of Britain. I happened, for instance, to notice a Bel stone marked on the ordnance map at the great hill fort of Eggardon in Dorset. Whether Eggardon was once Dun nan Each, the horse's fort, I do not know. This, however, seems possible, for the 'Grey Mare and her Colts' barrows are only five miles distant and the Grey Mare, or White Horse, played a great part in pre-Christian religion. The Saxons appear to have translated or distorted many ancient place names and in the process usually reversed the order of the words. Dun dubh became Blackburn and Cwm Bran Branscombe. Moridunum, Seaton, however retains its original order in translation from Muir dun. Both Gaelic and Welsh forms of Celtic are found in this area, which was once the borderland between the Durotriges and the Dumnonii.

To return to Lucifer. Lucifer was the bringer of the light. Everyone of course knew that the light came from the sun and so the sun and Lucifer are synonymous. Diana, in the Vangelo, created the light. Lucifer was her brother and lover. In Roman terms Lucifer is Apollo. In the Welsh lands Apollo was Mabon (or Maponus). Beelzebub, known to the Celts as Bel, Beli, Balor and so on, who burnt people up with his fiery glance, only another name for Lucifer or Lugh.

We have therefore a clear indication that the witch religion was not a single primitive belief derived from one Palaeolithic origin. It has one Great Mother, it is true, but Diana has at least two lovers to explain the union of two beliefs. In one the counterpart of the Great Mother is a nature god; in the other he is the sun. Having dissected these two beliefs out of it, we may at least suspect that there are others mixed up in it as well. For the moment, however, we will continue to investigate Lucifer and in this process find ourselves being led into some curious by-ways of study.

One of the best clues is Pope Gregory's instruction to the clergy that if they found beliefs which were so deeply rooted in pagan faith that they could not easily be removed, they were to turn them into Christian guise. This saved many things. Brigid, a form of the Great Mother, became a saint. So did Lugh and Mabon. Lugh apparently became Michael and Mabon became Andrew. This has been widely recognized for a long time and there is no need for me to try to explain how Lucifer became the very archangel Michael who, according to accepted belief, threw him out of Heaven on to earth. Both the Christian Church and the witches' Vangelo have this story of Lucifer being thrown out of Heaven. 'And there was war in Heaven,' says the Book of Revelation. 'Michael and his angels fought against the Dragon and his angels,' and goes on to say that the old Devil, Dragon, Serpent, or what not, was cast out and fell upon the earth. 'I beheld Lucifer as lightning fallen from Heaven.' In the Vangelo, Lucifer was cast out of Heaven for his pride in his beauty. The similarity between these two myths suggests that they are each derived from some yet more ancient religion.

Of course there is considerable confusion in all this, as might be expected when you try to adapt a belief from one faith to a totally different one. In Fig. 5 (5) I have drawn Michael from a gold 'angel' of Edward IV. There is seen Michael, winged and clad in scales. He has a fiery halo and is busy pushing a cross of Lorraine into the old Dragon's mouth. To make sure, however, that there should be no mistake, the artist who drew the design for the coin has put a small sun symbol beside the archangel's head. It had to be there, because there were two religions in the land. In the days of the Plantagenets, who, according to Dr. Margaret Murray, were all witches, the reverse of their silver coinage bears a representation of a cross with pellets, which could be taken either as a Christian cross or a pagan sun disc, whichever you preferred (Fig. 5 (3)).

If it had not been for the work of Margaret Murray, Sir James Fraser and Harold Bayley, we should probably never have thought of looking for evidence of this kind. We were brought up to the legacy of Victorian teaching, which gave the impression

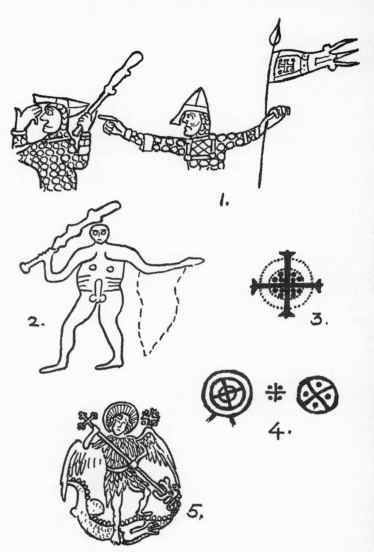

Fig. 5.

(1) Duke William at the battle of Hastings, showing his club and personal Standard with sun symbol. From the Bayeux Tapestry.

(2) The Cerne Giant (Helith, Helios, or Hercules) with his club.

(3) Sun symbol from a coin of Edward III.

(4) Bronze Age sun symbols from the Bohuslan rock engravings.

(5) St. Michael from a gold 'angel' of Edward IV showing sun symbol beside his head (actual figure is one inch long).

that Christianity had been the only religion in the land since the days when the pagan Northmen were tamed to it. There were a few old country people, of course, who still held to silly superstitions, but very few people grasped that these superstitions were surviving traces of a rival belief and still fewer who realized that this belief was not entirely extinct. If you wished to learn about paganism, you must either study the classics or go out to the lands where 'the heathen in his blindness bowed down to wood and stone'. The idea that one could learn about paganism amongst the people living in these islands never seems to have suggested itself to more than a minute number.

Our pagans do not seem to have gone in for much bowing down to images. Their religion was real paganism, in which living forces were worshipped with magical rites. They needed no images of the sun and moon, when they could see them in the sky; but only places in which to perform their nature magic. They did not even need statues of the Horned God, when they could hear the wild red stag's grunting roar in the dark autumn night. The powers of nature were all about them and they could portray them themselves in their seasonal festivities. It was the town-dweller in his rabbit warren of dirt and disease who, in his so-called cultured state, needed these images to bow down to. Some of the friction between Christianity and the witch cult in medieval times seems to me to have been due as much to the differences in outlook between townsman and countryman, as to any fundamental difference in the original teaching. In early medieval days members of ruling families appear to have had little difficulty in composing the differences and being members of both religions. Even the Christian priests and bishops were sometimes, as Margaret Murray has shown, called in to perform the pagan rites. It is easy to see how this came about. The king of the country or the priest in his parish was regarded as the professional go-between, whose business it was to ensure that the Higher Powers provided the community with prosperity and fertility of man, beast and field. It was useless to have a ruler or priest who did not see to this, and useless to have a god who took no interest in such matters, for they were the life of the people. Of what use was a moral code to an empty belly? It is one the two things which brook no denial. It was here that Pope Gregory's wise ordinance was most important. It was the dogmatist in the later medieval Church who, thinking himsel above such things, was responsible for the bitter campaign agains any form of diversionary belief. If organizations, like individuals are under the rule of Karma, as the Hindus believe, then these narrow churchmen have laid a bloody weight on the body they were supposed to serve. Had Gregory's rule been carried ou always, there would have been no reigns of massacre and murder

Remembering how important sacred places were in ancien religions and remembering Gregory's instruction, it seemed to me that there was an opportunity for learning something from the dedications of churches. Lugh being thought to be Michae and Mabon Andrew, it seemed to me that the topographica distribution of the churches dedicated to these two names migh possibly be instructive. It has always been conceded by anti quarians that early churches were frequently placed on sites formerly devoted to pagan rites. If the distribution of the churches could be linked to any known prehistoric sites, then the probability was that the people using the prehistoric site also used the spot on which the church now stands for some perfor mance of a pagan religious nature. I had no idea what was likely to emerge from such a study; nor whether it had been attempted by anyone else. Being, however, an archaeologist, it seemed to me that no harm could come from investigating. I would look up the dedications to Michael and Andrew for a given area, plot them on a map and see whether they were entirely sporadic or distributed in relation to something we already recognized as being a prehistoric phenomenon.

It was obvious of course that some dedications were quite modern, some wrongly ascribed and some unknown. But with this proviso, the investigation appeared to be fairly reliable There remained, however, a problem. How close was a pre historic religious site to a prehistoric dwelling site? There was no means of answering this, but I decided that an hour's walk or three miles over unfenced or unwalled country was a reasonable measure of propinquity. I soon saw that the bulk of correspond ing situations were well within this limit and that a few at ar hour and a half to two hours' walk probably belonged to the pattern of distribution.

The story begins with the borrowing of a copy of Crockford Most people have never met Crockford except in novels

Crockford's Clerical Directory is something like Lloyd's Register of Shipping, but not so clearly printed and less vital to Britain. If you have seen neither, it is something like several telephone directories bound together. Crockford gives a list of churches with their dedications, incumbents, whom we should call 'parsons', dioceses and so on. I am told it is not reliable as far as the dedications go; but it is as good as anything one can lay hands on without considerable trouble. Some of the dioceses have obviously been better handled than others. Personally I would rather have Lloyd's Register every time: Sarah Jane. Wood barquentine. Built 1873. Two hundred tons, and so on (this is not a real one), tells you a lot if you love ships, but Crockford has a smell of death and decaying vegetation in cold churches. Still, it is useful for our purposes. It is a tedious business wading through Crockford to find the dedications. They are arranged in alphabetical order in very small print. Unless the light is very good, you need a lens to read them.

I wanted the churches in three dioceses of which I knew the topography reasonably well, namely Exeter, Sarum and Bath and Wells. Those of Devon have been very kindly checked for me by Miss Theo Brown, the folk-lorist. Sarum and Bath and Wells are unchecked and from Crockford. As far as I can judge, Sarum has been treated with less care than the other two. Many dedications are not even suggested.

There are about forty-five Michaels in Devon and only twenty-nine Andrews, several of these are only those of small coastal or hill-top chapels. According to Crockford, there are twenty-nine Michaels in the large Sarum diocese and forty in Bath and Wells. As I was six short from Crockford for Devon, it is probably safe to add a few to each of the other dioceses. In any case the two combined are but a small proportion of the total number of village churches. By far the largest number are those of the Virgin Mary, who we will mention again later. According to Crockford there are at least 525 churches in the Exeter diocese, 509 in Bath and Wells and 556 in Salisbury, which gives an idea of what a small percentage of the whole number is taken up by Michael and Andrew. It works out at about a fourteenth of the total for Michael.

Now the actual dwelling-places of the peoples of the prehistoric Iron Age, the age of the Celts, are few and far between, for they are not easily recognized. The strongholds of the chieftains, however, the duns, or hill forts, are mostly known. There the people presumably hurried in time of trouble. In them the head of the clan, or the chief of the sept, presumably had his home and there his wives and servants lived more or less permanently. He himself, if we may judge from the Irish epic stories, was frequently away hunting, guesting or fighting. One would expect the sacred places of the community to have been reasonably close to the hill fort; although some were no doubt of such sanctity that they were known over wide areas and may not have been anywhere near a dun. Some of these may well have been of much greater antiquity than the Iron Age and, like Stonehenge and Avebury, in use for many centuries already. It seems reasonable then to suppose that, if we can demonstrate a relationship between the Iron Age duns and the dedications to Michael and Andrew, we are really demonstrating the relationship between the dun and the sacred places formerly connected with it. Whether these places were once springs, wells, trees or stones is of no importance to the general investigation at this juncture.

With our list of dedications beside us, a pair of dividers and a ruler and with the ordnance map spread out on the table, it becomes clear at once that a very large proportion of Michaels and Andrews are within an hour's walk of well-known Iron Age hill forts. It is quite surprising. You find large areas with no duns and no Michaels or Andrews. Then an area studded with forts in which the required dedications are frequent. Often, as at Musbury and Axmouth in the Axe valley, the village churches are just at the feet of the hills on which the duns of Musbury and Hawksdown stand. At Montacute there is not even a church and the dun itself is known as St. Michael's Hill. Twenty hill forts in the Salisbury diocese have a required dedication within an hour's walk. Some, like Musbury in Wiltshire, have two Michaels; others, like Clearbury ring, have both Michael and Andrew. The map (Fig. 6) gives some idea of the picture for the are between the Wiltshire Avon and Bridgwater Bay. The assume relationship appears to hold good from Cambridge to Sta Point.

It seems to me that without further ado we can make a number of inferences from this little piece of research work. We can say that in many cases Michael and Andrew do appear to be linked to the Iron Age duns. If so, it seems reasonable to conclude that the folk-lore pioneers were right when they said that these two saints were once Lugh and Mabon. Then we have surely a picture of continuity over a period of two thousand

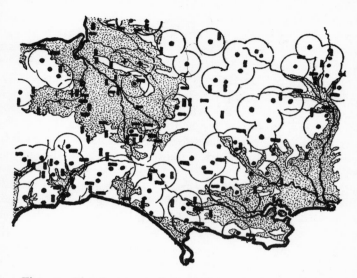

Fig. 6. Sketch map of South-west England between Bridgwater Bay and the Wiltshire Avon, showing hill forts as a dot with a surrounding three-mile circle, lake villages with a central cross, dedications to Michael as a vertical stroke and to Andrew as a horizontal one.

years, which makes nonsense of the Victorian idea that the Anglo-Saxons displaced or destroyed the bulk of the earlier population. I have made this suggestion frequently before, basing it on other evidence, but this continuity in the use of sacred rites is as good an argument as any I have yet found. When the Christian teachers came among the supposedly Anglo-Saxon population, they met people all over the southern half of Britain so determined to reverence numerous Celtic places that they found it necessary to invoke Gregory's instruction by twisting Lugh into Michael and Mabon into Andrew. Anglo-Saxon deities that are known, Woden, Nerthus and the rest, bear little resemblance to Lugh and Mabon. Nerthus is probably the Great Mother, but it would be a matter of great difficulty to decide which, if any, Saxon god represented the sun. Yet when King Cnut made a law against pagan customs, he specially mentioned the sun and moon, springs and trees. It looks very much as if he were legislating against the witch religion, in which both of Diana's lovers were involved. The sun was Lucifer, the moon Diana, while the trees and springs were the properties of Pan. It is a strange thought that, while sitting in a pew in a country church, you are sitting on the spot where, two thousand years before, the congregation feasted and danced in honour of Lucifer and Diana. Yet perhaps it is not so strange after all, for the site which was thus wrested from one old religion was later forcibly taken from the Roman Catholics.

This study could, I feel certain, be greatly elaborated. If somebody with time to spare would take some of these hill forts and examine all the field names in the neighbourhood, clues will still be available, a Lugmoor, an Ogwell and so on. The Celts were in the habit of giving names to any feature in the countryside which might be useful for reference in conversation or direction, the speckled knoll, the polecat's crag, the raven's rock and so on. Many were translated into Anglo-Saxon, or pidgin-German, and some at least remain in field names to this day. If an area where one clue to the ancient religion is known to exist is carefully examined and all folk stories connected with it are also collected, a picture will begin to form. When a group of several such areas is examined as a whole, it will be found that quite a lot of information comes to light. I have already made some attempt at this kind of thing in relation to the figures at Wandlebury near Cambridge (see *Gogmagog*), here in Branscombe and round Moretonhampstead, but am well aware that my investigations have been far too superficial. Enquiries in the west of England, where there are ghosts innumerable, black dogs, and stories of queer happenings like coffins lying in the road at night; where half-cloaked Celtic names abound and

Saxon immigration was relatively slight, should produce evidence quite as valuable and interesting as any digging of the entrances of hill forts. Strange as it may seem, little attempt has been made to find the houses of the chieftains inside the hill forts, for archaeologists are mostly like sheep. If one digs the entrance to a camp, all must do so. Better work has been done in Ireland, where the homes inside have often been carefully examined.

Chapter Five

LUCIFER now has been brought back into the light and we can leave him for the moment and study the other form of him given in the witch trials, Beelzebub.

> Here come I, old Beelzebub,
>   And in one hand I carry a club.
> And in the other a frying-pan,
>   And I think myself a jolly old man.

This was a traditional doggerel rhyme collected at Cerne Abbas at the foot of the turf-cut giant and referring to him. Beelzebub was found in the New Testament as was Lucifer. It was translated as King, or Lord, of the Flies, which may or may not be correct, for Beelzebub was 'prince of the devils' and a devil originally meant a holy one, as the word 'divus' means in Latin and 'deva' means in India today. But the gods of one religion are the devils of another and they are liable to changes in fortune like anybody else. Divine and devilish are the same thing. It depends on how you view them. But Beelzebub was a very ancient personage in the Near East. He was originally Bel, or Baal, which some authorities think to have been an ancient Hittite word akin to Celtic. One imagines that Bel means beautiful; although it is usually taken to mean lord or god. It is not the personal name of the god, but a title. Baalim were little Baals, presumably statues, or perhaps stone phalli. Ashtoreth, Astarte, Ishtah and so Artemis, the Queen of Heaven, that is the Diana whom we are looking for, was Baal's consort. Now it happens that we know how Baal was portrayed in the ancient world, for when Hiram, king of Tyre, built his famous temple in the days of King Solomon (that is somewhere about 900 B.C.), he put up a statue to Baal. The statue is said to have been like a figure of Hercules, with a club. This was all long before the Galatae, the Gauls, passed over into Asia Minor and still longer before St. Paul wrote them an Epistle, so if Baal was of Celtic origin, he belonged to some much earlier wave of invaders. But who knows who the Keltoi, or Galatae, really were? They were certainly not the little dark men, who people speak of as Celts today. All classical writers and all their own writings speak of them as tall fair men. The fallen Galatian warriors on the sculptures of Pergamon show men of this type, who might easily pass for brigadiers in the British Army today. Everyone must know the famous statue of the dying Gaul, and I need say no more about it. The point, however, is this: if Baal came to Asia Minor with some Celtic people before the days of King Solomon, he probably reached Britain before the days of the Celtic Iron Age also. This means that some Bronze Age peoples in Britain were an earlier wave of Celts than the iron-users, who do not seem to have arrived here much before 400 B.C.

Baal is known in place names in England, but in Wales and Ireland he has a considerable place in literature. He was known as Beli and Balor, but like all these gods he had a large number of different names as well. He was certainly Dagda, who was a typical club-bearing Hercules. He was Ogmius to the Gauls of France and in Ireland the form of writing known as 'ogham' still bears his name. To those who do not know the term, ogham writing is a system of straight cuts formed on the angle of the side of a stone or piece of wood. It resembles the cuts made on a tally stick. Ogham writing is supposedly understood, but it is remarkable with what frequency ogham experts differ in their translation of a particular inscription.

Balor was obviously the sun. He had a glance which burnt people up and, in this respect, resembled the Indian god Siva. There are so many ways in which the Indian gods agree with those of western Europe, even to their sitting in the 'lotus' position, that it is impossible to evade the conclusion that both are derived from some original Aryan source. This fact brings us again to the idea of waves of diffusion spreading in many directions, well before the days of King Solomon. One thinks at once of Homer's Achaeans who, as the late Sir William Ridgeway demonstrated so clearly in his *Early Age of Greece*, had all the characteristics of a north European people. They had obviously been settled in Greece for some time before Homer wrote in about 1000 B.C. We can begin to see not only why the Greek myths should resemble those of western Europe, but also that we should look for the appearance of Celtic gods in Britain well back in time before the days of iron. With the Celtic gods, we should expect surely an early form of Celtic speech to have been in use. This has a number of drastic implications for the pre-historian and makes 'overhanging rim urns' and 'carp's tongue swords' seem rather small beer. We can see how right Sir Cyril Fox was to concentrate on such traces of ritual as he could observe in the burial cairns he excavated.

Here then we seem to have one of the ripples I mentioned before. A ring spreading out from some unknown source and washing up on different shores in approximately the order of its distance from its place of origin. It reached Greece before 1000 B.C., Palestine well before 900 B.C. and perhaps before 1400 B.C., India maybe a little later. When did it reach England? Here we can only make a guess, but looking at the orthodox archaeological work of the late Professor Gordon Childe and the efforts of more recent workers, such as Professor Stuart Piggott, I feel that, presuming that their dating is reasonably good, the uniform spread of the Middle Bronze Age culture wide about the land somewhere about 1400 B.C. may well be an indication of this, shall we call it 'proto-Celtic' spread. It may have arrived earlier. The so-called 'Beaker' people could have brought it about 1800 B.C., but I do not like the shape of their heads!

Their skulls are round and one would expect the proto-Celt to have had a skull of medium length. Unfortunately the Middle Bronze Age people cremated their dead, probably in honour of some supposed command from Beelzebub himself, and we can have no idea what shape their skulls may have been. Otherwise there is much to commend the Beaker people as candidates. They were sturdy, migrant pastoralists, apparently driving their flocks and herds for long distances across the downs and moorland ridges. They seem to have been the originators of the solar-disc stone circles which still stud the countryside today. On the whole I think the Beaker people must have been our earliest proto-Celtic wave. If so, then since their Baal appears to have reached Britain before he reached the Near East, we should look for the origin of our ripple at no great distance. The Beaker

58

people are often thought to have come from somewhere near the foothills of the Alps and are spoken of as an Alpine race. This would suit the time to distance ratio very well. I think our Beaker friends spoke Gaelic. By this I do not mean, of course, that a Beaker man could stand on the quay at Mallaig and indulge in a long conversation with a MacDonald from South Uist. The Gaelic of today seems to me to bear much the same relationship to a lost original that modern English bears to Old German. Both these modern tongues are a kind of pidgin language, which has passed through many mouths which were brought up to another speech. The Beaker man, if I am right in thinking he used it, spoke Gaelic with a much more elaborate grammar; but in this language many words would be recognizable today.

There are now believed to have been two distinct strains of Beaker man. One is thought to have come by sea from the south up the Atlantic seaboard. We are not dealing with this branch now. The other is brought into eastern England by way of the vanished plains, which are now submerged beneath the North Sea. These men should have been our proto-Celtic wave.

The users of iron, who seem to have formed a second wave of true Celts, appear to have begun to settle in eastern England somewhere about 400 B.C. If we can trust bardic tradition, and I think we can do so, it gives a similar date to that arrived at by archaeological study. The Cwmry, as the bards sang, arrived about the Humber under the leadership of Hu the Mighty. Hu was clearly a kind of Brahma, having no visible form and being omnipotent. He is quite distinct from the family affairs of Lugh and Mabon, but it seems probable that the Druids and bards absorbed the earlier gods into their teaching in the same way that Lugh and Mabon were absorbed into Christianity. The conception of Hu and the ideas of transmigration which went with it were far too difficult for comprehension by the ordinary tribesman.

To return to Beelzebub, we will look at some of the other information we have about Baal or Bel. The Carthaginians took him with them into Africa and there, as Baal Hammon, he had a consort Tanit. Tanit is no doubt our Tana of the Vangelo. Baal Hammon at Carthage was a horned god. The pair were the great male and female principles. Baal, as Balor in Ireland, was, as I have said before, the representation of the sun and like Lucifer he was worsted in combat by a later version of the same theme. Just as Lucifer is said to have been defeated by Michael, so was Balor blinded by Lugh in his single eye. This was a primitive explanation of how the old sun god came to be replaced by a more cultured specimen. Lugh is simply a more advanced Balor. When we find a Bel stone at Eggardon Iron Age fort, with two churches dedicated to St. Michael near it, we have a picture of an evolutionary process drawn for us on the ordnance map. Lugh, Bel and Dagda are all linked together in various ways. Dagda and Bel are each in some phase a Hercules figure, with a club, and the day on which Dagda was traditionally forced to eat a huge meal out of a hole in the ground was Lugh's great festival of Lugnasad (1 November). In other words Lugh's festival was once the day of Dagda's feast. The more primitive version of the god with his club had been replaced with one armed with spear and sling. It seems probable that each version formerly belonged to a different tribe. The same multiplicity of names will be noticed when we come to deal with their consorts. It is unfortunate that the name of Balor's female counterpart appears to have been lost; but since that of Baal Hammon was Tanit, which must surely be a form of Tana or Diana, it seems evident that it was Danu or Annu, the great Irish Mother Goddess, whose breasts are still to be seen rising above the fertile plains.

It is as certain as most things in this type of study that the real name of any god was never mentioned in public. Baal in whatever form the word occurs simply means god, or lord, or something of the sort. Similarly with Dagda, who is usually referred to as 'the Dagda'; this will not be his secret name. I believe it to be no more or less than Dada, Dad, Daddy and the rest of the children's names for father. It is exactly comparable to Pa, Papa and so on. Dagda was simply 'the Great Father'. Baal, Balor, Beli, Beelzebub and the other forms were just 'the Lord'. Lugh and Lucifer are 'the Light'. None of these is the god's name and there is nothing to prevent any or all of the terms applying to the same deity. It was the gradual coalescing of tribes into nations which led to the splitting up of one god into many. To some it was the fatherhood that appealed and he was Dagda. To others his power, and he was known as Lord. To a third group his bringing of sunlight appeared to be most important. The larger the nation became and the more tribes it came to include, the more numerous its gods would be. Rome had them by the score and yet they were apparently all derived from one original idea of a Great Father and Great Mother. Seton Lloyd in his excavations in Turkey found a succession of superimposed temples covering a thousand years of Bronze Age, in which the symbolism of male and female fertility was presented with great simplicity and without change. The horned altar to which the sacrifice was bound, as it says in the Bible, was found in the earliest temples right through to the latest. The gods worshipped there were probably known as Baal and Ashtoreth.

It may be thought that I am simplifying everything too much, but has there really been any change at all in 4,000 years? 'No man hath seen God at any time' holds as good today as it did to the Beaker shepherd standing where Chanctonbury Ring was still fifteen hundred years away in the future. If you are going to personify the Deity, it seems more reasonable to have both male and female, as the Roman Catholics now seem to have appreciated. The druidic conception of Hu the Mighty, who was so small as to be invisible and yet omnipotent, was of a different order altogether. To regard the Iron Age Celts, who had attained to this degree of thinking, as blue-painted savages is quite ridiculous. People in western Europe are only just beginning to reach this stage again. Men, so the Druids taught, must be born and suffer again and again until they are fit to stand the strain of Eternity. The anthropomorphic creeds whisked them away at once after death to lead a useless existence of lolling about, feasting and flirting in a land of perpetual youth, or more boring still of standing about singing hymns for ever. Give me Hu the Mighty every time; I can see some sense in this idea.

The religion of the witches today certainly appears to have some druidic tenets. They believe that after death they will be born again. If they can get Diana to intercede for them, they will be born again surrounded by those they loved in this life. This belief bears a close resemblance to the ideas of those students of the occult today who accept the reliability of evidence supposedly derived through mediums from persons in the next world. A good summary of these ideas can be found in Dr. Raynor C. Johnson's *Imprisoned Splendour*. A comparison between Druidism, the witch beliefs, Brahminism and psychic studies strongly suggests that all were obtained in the same manner. The original teachings of Christ and Buddha, stripped of the later dogma which has grown up round these teachings, may well belong to the same group. In fact, one fundamental belief seems to be common to all. If we can stand back far enough from the chatter of the world, it is easy to regard all these faiths as warring sects of one universal belief.

In witch belief it is the Lord of the Underworld, a kind of Hades or Pluto, who decides on the circumstances in which people shall be born again. Unfortunately I do not know his name. I happen to have been told the name under which the modern witches adore Diana, but since they are not supposed to divulge it, I think it would be unfair to mention it here. Their reticence, however, seems to me to be unnecessary, for it does not appear to be the secret name of the goddess. It seems to translate without difficulty from a garbled Celtic into 'The Lady of the Summer Pastures'. No one could use it to work magic against her. We find exactly the same type of phraseology used in pagan times in Britain to describe the Great Mother. She is called 'Macha', the 'Lady of the Fertile Plain' and 'Cailleach', the 'Lady of the Forest'.

Beelzebub is getting left out again. It is so easy to digress in this subject. Baal then, over much of the ancient world, was a rude Father God with a club. Somebody described him as a rustic Hercules. I have to thank the Deputy Serjeant at Arms of the House of Commons for putting me on to an interesting line of inquiry. He wrote to ask me whether I could suggest a relationship between the Great Mace in the House of Commons and the mace shown in the hand of Duke William, William the Conqueror, on the Bayeaux Tapestry (Fig. 5 (1)). Of course I had never thought that there could be any connection, but once the suggestion was made, the answer did not appear to be very difficult. Duke William's father was Robert the Devil. This does not mean that he beat his wife or cheated over money. It means that he was a living representative of Lucifer, or Beelzebub, probably over the whole of Normandy. He was the Devil to the Christian priests. William the Conqueror was not born in holy wedlock, but was known as The Bastard. As living representative of the god, he carried Baal's distinguishing emblem, the club, and this is what is shown in his son's hand.[1] It is a symbol

[1] His standard also is a pennon bearing a sun symbol.

of delegated divine authority. Dagda's club was so big that it had to be borne on wheels and needed eight men to carry it. This is what the mace in the House of Commons represents. It shows that the king had delegated his divine power of lawgiver to the members assembled in Parliament, or rather, I think I am right in saying, to his representative the Serjeant at Arms; without the mace the laws they passed were without authority. Parliament was by no means the only body to whom such power was delegated. Generals and admirals were presented with a baton by the king, not only in England, but in France also. Authority to command was passed right down from the god to the king, to the war leader and even to the tipstaff and police constable. It is probably the most dramatic survival of paganism in existence. The constable's truncheon perhaps owes its handy size and shape to the belaying pin, snatched from the pin-rail of a vessel in time of trouble, but it is a symbol of delegated authority none the less. It used to be elaborately painted with civic arms, the power having been delegated by the king to the civic authority by charter and from this to the constable. Two thousand years or so have passed since men carved Beelzebub's giant figure in the turf at Cerne Abbas (Fig. 5 (2)) and still today men are walking our streets carrying the image of his club. Rightly indeed did Kipling describe England as 'Merlin's Island of Grammerie' when such things are perpetuated here.

I have talked about the Cerne Giant at some length in *Gogmagog*, but we cannot leave him out of this discussion. He is a veritable Hercules figure, a true Baal. Two hundred feet of him strides down the hillside, powerful and immodest, waving his monstrous club. No such picture of masculinity is known in Europe. Dagda is regarded as crude, but he at least wore a tunic, hood and sandals; while the Cerne Giant appears nude and proud of it. By chance the local name of the Cerne Baal seems to have been preserved in the thirteenth-century chronicle of Walter of Coventry. It was Helith. This name resembles so closely that of the Greek sun Helios that we can be reasonably certain that it had the same meaning. If so, the 'Hele' names from Suffolk and Essex to Stonehenge and Exeter all refer to him. The hill of Health, the Heel Stone and Helions Bumpstead are a few examples. Helions Bumpstead incidentally has a dedication to St. Andrew, who in the east of the country seems to be more popular than Michael. If it be objected that these Hele names refer to some holy place, what could be more holy than a site dedicated to a great god? Hell itself, where the wicked souls were tormented in perpetual fire, seems pretty close to the flash of Balor's eye. I hope that somebody who lives near Helions Bumpstead will make an intensive search of that area for clues in field names and folk tales, to see whether more cannot be learnt. It may be more than a coincidence that a parson from one of the nearby villages recently informed me that witches were still numerous in his parish. As he told me he was well acquainted with the Cerne Giant and the stories connected with it, I felt he was probably right about the witches also. Whether they are groups of witches organized in covens, or just isolated women with a smattering of the old lore, we cannot tell. The religion is secret. Nearer the East Anglian coast at least one coven still exists. As I do not know its exact location, I cannot say whether Michael, Andrew or Hele is to be found there; but, if it is where I think it is, there is an Andrew within the qualifying hour's walk.

Some Devils, whatever their names may be, carried a sword and shield. Some months ago Mr. N. Hudleston, the folk-lorist, sent me a photograph of the Devil's Stone at Copgrove church, near Ripon in Yorkshire, and asked me who I thought was represented by this figure with its enormous phallus. It is only fair to him to add that when the photograph was shown to another expert, he interpreted the object in question as being a portion of the female anatomy. The photograph shows a very worn carving from which I have drawn what I think I can see on Fig. 4 (a). It is easy to understand why it is still known as the Devil's Stone, for it appears to be horned and carries both sword and shield in the wrong hands. The Devil in popular tradition in eastern England is left-handed. From this comes the old saying of a 'left-handed gift'. The debatable object appears to me to be the scabbard of his sword and I know no chape, that is the protective end to the scabbard, shown or found on any sword of later date than the Early Iron Age which remotely resembles this one. The horns too are like the horns frequently found on pictures of male heads in the Celtic art of the Continent (Fig. 4 (b)).

I do not think the carving dates from the Anglo-Saxon period to which many such carvings found in churches belong. It seems rather to be an exceedingly rare example of Celtic work and probably of the first century A.D. If that is so, it may well be a Cernunnus, although all known pictures of him have a stag's antlers on the head. But the Carthaginian Baal was horned. I am inclined to call the figure Nuada of the Silver Arm, who was ruler of the Irish gods and overlord of Lugh, until he lost his arm in battle and was succeeded by Lugh. But in the Welsh stories, Lugh and Nuada, known as Lud and Nud, are apparently identical and both have a silver hand. It is probable then that we have one of the frequent cases in Celtic mythology where one god, or goddess, is represented in three phases, or persons. Our Copgrove figure would then be a form of Lugh. Having got as far as this, arguing to myself, I picked Crockford off the floor and looked up the dedication of the church. By this time I was no longer surprised at the coincidence; Copgrove church is dedicated to Michael. This is, I think, the first case in which we have a hint of the form once taken by the sacred pagan site. I do not know the age of the name, but surely it suggests that the original shrine was a clump of trees. Here again we have a case where careful local research might yield considerable fresh information.

Chapter Six

LUCIFER and Pan were two of Diana's lovers and through the course of time their qualities and attributes became mixed. According to Dr. Gardner, however, the modern witches pay the greatest reverence to a third. This god's name is not revealed, but he is Lord of the Underworld. It is not quite clear whether the modern witches distinguish between Diana and her daughter, Aradia, in the way that the Italian witches did. In fact the daughter seems to have dropped out of the modern ritual. She would have been only one aspect of the Great Mother in any case. Whether then it is Diana or Aradia who goes to visit the Lord of the Underworld, is not a great matter. One of them went and after being divested of her clothing by the guards of the seven gates, in a manner which suggests to Dr. Gardner the Dance of the Seven Veils, is greeted by the Lord of the Underworld, scourged and made his mistress. This myth must be a variant of that of Ceres, Pluto and Proserpina and is known in one form or another all over the ancient world. It is a myth representing the change of the seasons. It is curious, however, that Diana, the Queen of Night, should be mated with the Lord of Darkness and one would think that there had been some confusion here. The whole object of the union was to bring about the return of fertility in the spring of the coming year. Light and Darkness should have been lovers, not Dark and Dark. I think the answer must be that there was once only one god of Darkness and that was female, an aspect of the Great Mother. With the change to male gods, however, there were two and these had to be mated to make sense of an impossible situation. Diana now intercedes for her votaries with the Lord of Darkness, who arranges for their rebirth under conditions pleasing to his mistress. At one time she would have seen to all this herself. The

Lord of Darkness is a newcomer, pointing to a different stage reached in an ancient belief.

The modern witches speak of this god as 'Lord of life in death'. He is thus comparable with the Indian Siva (Fig. 7 (b)) who is lord both of fertility and of death. In the same way Kali (Fig. 7 (a)), one of Siva's wives, is murderous and comparable with the Celtic Cailleach.

We have some difficulty in identifying a Celtic god who was sole Lord of the Underworld. In fact the Celtic belief in an Underworld seems to be somewhat vague. There is a much clearer picture of Tir nan Og, the happy land of youth, over the Western Ocean and beyond the Sunset. This may represent a true Otherworld, but I am by no means convinced that it is not a legend relating to early crossings of the Atlantic Ocean. There is a Welsh Hades, Cythraul, or the Abyss. This Abyss, however, according to the Mabinogion, had three successive rulers, Arawn, Pwyll and his son, Pryderi. Pwyll is spoken of as Lord, or Head, of Annwn and was married to Rhiannon, a Great Mother goddess, in the correct manner. The whole matter is, however, far from clear. Pwyll,

Fig. 7. (a) Kali, (b) Siva, from Indian bronzes. Note Kali's garland of human heads, the skulls, snakes, and that each figure has a 'third eye'.

with his yellow-headed white hell-hounds, may be the best candidate and we can link him up with a more famous king of all the British gods.

Sir Mortimer Wheeler, who has great skill in choosing suitable places for excavation, once explored a Romano-British temple on a hill at Lydney in Gloucestershire, which went a long way towards destroying the accepted picture of Roman Britain becoming an economic derelict in the second half of the fourth century. The big temple appears to have been built after the great invasion of Britain by Picts, Scots and Saxons in 366 or 367. The temple was that of Nodens, who is a figure we know already. Nodens is Nuada of the Silver Hand, who was king of the Irish gods, in what we may call the second stage of belief, when Dagda was still there but the gods had become more cultured. Nuada is Nudd in the Welsh form of the name, but he is also 'Ludd law ereint', Ludd of the Silver Hand. Ludd is clearly Lugh of the Irish Tales, but he is also then Nuada with his silver hand. The temple of Nodens is thus a temple of Lugh.

There are two remarkable things about the Lydney temple, both exceeding the importance of the lateness of its date. In the first place there was a remarkable number of representations of dogs. One of these has a human face, while a second is a really fine bronze casting of a wolf-hound. These votive dogs did not come there by accident. They were offerings to a god who regarded dogs as of special importance and presumably owned hounds himself.

The second point is the character of the building itself. It is not built in the ordinary Classical form of a sacred inner building surrounded by cloisters. It is more in the form of a great hall surrounded by alcoves, or bays. Sir Mortimer in his report suggests, no doubt rightly, that these bays were intended for people to take the sacred temple sleep. Nodens then was Lord of the Land of Sleep, childhood's 'Land of Nod', or Nudd. And he was a lord of hounds. It seems pretty clear that he is the same as Pwyll, Lord of Annwn.

Fabulous dogs are not really our concern here and I know that they are being intensively studied by my friend, Miss Theo Brown, but we cannot leave this part of the story without paying them some attention. Ghost dogs are mostly black. Some are friendly and protective: others are bringers of terrible misfortune and death. The Barguest, presumably the burghgeist, of eastern England is of this kind and so are some of the Black Dogs of Devon. Those of Lincolnshire, however, are protective. The phantom dogs of the Western Isles and apparently those of east Devon are like Pwyll's hounds, white with yellow on their heads. All these manifestations are like the Loch Ness monster, some people see them, others do not. Those who have not seen them are told by faith that there could be no such things and flatly refuse to take the slightest interest in the words of apparently credible witnesses. I know people who have seen the Loch Ness monster and apparitions of the Black Dogs and have no reason to suppose that their eyesight was faulty or that they were not telling the truth. These are phenomena which people see and are not the product of hangovers from whisky, nor the result of tricks of light. Most black dogs are seen at night and they are heard also. I do not know the explanation, but am convinced that when it is found, it will be in accordance with a law of nature, even if this law has not yet been formulated.

There is a ghost white dog reported from the lane outside this house of Hole where I am writing. At least four people claim to have seen it in recent years, without any previous knowledge that it was supposed to be there. When we had just moved in here three years ago, my wife and I noticed a large white dog standing at the gate and looking in in a friendly manner. It was a collie, with streaks of yellow on its head and neck. I asked my tenant, who farms the surrounding land, whose dog it was and he replied that there was no dog like that for miles around. We have no dog. We have not seen the white dog again.

Here you have a story which is of no importance, but there is a sequel and I think it needs some explanation other than coincidence. Some months later when the vegetation, born of years of neglect, on the slope below this house died down, I found an open trench cut into the hill for the foundations of a shed. As I never neglect the chance of looking at a section which might produce archaeological information, I got down into it and examined its sides. There were numerous animal bones sticking out, some bits of medieval pottery, which might have been expected since the site is known to have been occupied since the beginning of the thirteenth century, and a fragment of a glazed floor-tile. At a guess this tile dates from about 1350. On the tile was stamped a large part of the body of a white dog. Since that time I have spent many hours digging away at the side of the trench with a trowel in the hope of finding enough pieces of tile to make up the whole picture. I have found many interesting things, which need not be enumerated now, and a large number of small pieces of tile. I never find a large piece and have never found the complete picture, but I have most of it (Fig. 8). The tiles fitted together on the floor of a building, I think of a private mortuary chapel. They formed a pattern of white circles

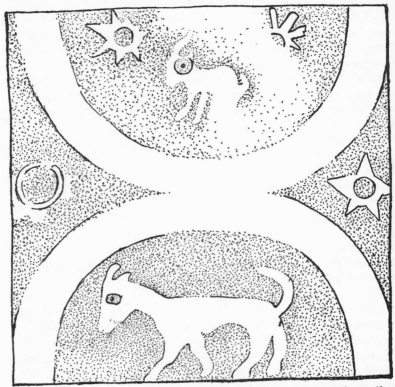

Fig. 8. Reconstruction of floor-tile from Hole, Branscombe. These tiles were first stamped with a wooden die; the design was then roughly painted in white and lastly covered with pale olive-green glaze. The tiles are approximately $6\frac{1}{4}$ in. square and probably mid-fourteenth century in date. Reconstructed from fragments of six tiles.

on a green background. In one half of the circle was a white dog and in the other a white hare, flanked by the sun and moon symbols. I cannot find anyone who knows this type of tile, but the dog and hare is a very common theme in Romano-British art. Innumerable handles of pocket knives found all over the country have it on them. The hare is the commonest type of animal into which a witch is supposed to be able to change and in which form she could only be killed by a silver bullet. It is thought by some psychologists to be a symbol of the psyche, or soul, and is known to have been a creature of the moon goddess. What of the white dog? On the tile he is much larger and more important than the hare. If she represents the moon, then surely he represents the sun. Both symbols are found on the tile. Does it not seem probable that the tiles were set in the chapel by people who were devotees of both the old and the new religions? We know who they were and the hare and the dog do not occur on their armorial bearings. That Christianity and the Dianic cult both existed in Devon in the fourteenth century is shown by the Bishop's Register of Exeter. The bishop found the monks of Frithelstock Priory worshipping a statue like 'the unchaste' Diana at an altar in the woods and made them destroy it.

Now a student of solid fact, a scientist, will see no connection between the tiles with their white dogs and the ghost white dog in the lane. But there may be a real connection. If we may trust some of the theories evolved by those who study psychical research, then some people can produce phantasms at will in the same general way as television pictures are produced. Others can see these phantasms as apparently real objects. We can see a possibility that when the Holcombs sold Hole to the Bartletts in 1605, or when the chapel was destroyed by fire, as I infer from the information I have gleaned by excavation, somebody thought with sufficient force and visualized 'the white dog of the Holcombs will haunt the place now'. And so it did. I do not believe necessarily that this is what happened, but I do not deny the possibility. No one has done enough work on these subjects to produce a reliable answer. Whether it is the correct answer or not does not matter to our study, but the tiles do. They point clearly to the white dogs of Pwyll, or Nodens, still being remembered and regarded as important in the fourteenth century and to their relationship with the sun still being understood.

The belief in the Black Dog is very prevalent in East Anglia and it is usually known as a shuck, or ghost. On the coast of Norfolk, however, as we learn from the late W. A. Duff in *Highways and Byways of East Anglia*, it was known as Moddy Dhoo. This adds to the evidence which suggests that the Iceni

71

were 'Q' Celts, speaking a form of Gaelic. Moddy Dhoo is the Gaelic Madadh Dubh, Black Dog, and thus presumably 2,000 years old.

I will give one other instance of the appearance of a phantom dog. This time it was a large black one. Parson Thornton, whose fascinating *Reminiscences of an Old Devonshire Clergyman* is well worth reading for the clear picture it gives of the Devon country life of about a hundred years ago, was a great disbeliever in ghosts and suchlike phenomena. As a young man he was at Selworthy, a little village between Porlock and the sea, where conditions were very simple. One day a large black dog rushed past a woman, who was much upset by the incident. Thornton hurried to calm her down, and on the way back fell into conversation with the sexton. 'I know all about it,' said the sexton and went on to explain his knowledge. He said that a coffin with a woman's body in it was being carried to the church yard for burial. On the way one of the coffin-handles came loose. The sexton picked up a stone and hammered it tight. He believed that the point on the shank of the coffin-handle had pierced the woman's skull and let her spirit out. The sexton knew all about it and so thought he knew the connection between the ghost dog and the woman's spirit. What this connection was we shall have to guess. There seem to be two possibilities. The first is that the sexton believed in the druidic idea of the transmigration of souls. In this case he thought that the woman's soul had been reincarnated in the body of a black dog. The second idea is that the black dog had been sent by the Lord of the Underworld to fetch away the woman's soul. Other Devon stories of the effect on elderly or sick persons of seeing black dogs suggests that the second idea is the correct one. According to the witches' Vangelo Diana used a dog as a messenger. It will be most interesting to see what Theo Brown makes of this problem. In any case we have in this Selworthy story, reported by an unimpeachable witness, a case of dual beliefs being held by a man who had position of some standing in a Christian community.

The Lord of the Underworld is of course common to many religions and in some cases appears to have been a god of the Upper levels, who became pushed down to look after the affairs of the dead when his devotees were conquered by another race. In Indian theology Vishnu is believed to have trodden Bali, the

72

honest king of the Demons, into some kind of infernal regions. Bali, who was obviously a god of this earth before the misfortune overtook him, is probably our Balor, or Baal, and was therefore the sun god of one race demoted by a succeeding people. This theme runs right through our investigations. If we knew the name of the witches' Lord of the Underworld, we might well find that it was the same Beelzebub mentioned in the witch trials.

The Lord of the Underworld, as I have said, as such does not figure much in our Celtic mythology, except the Welsh Arawn, Pwyll, and Pryderi, his son, who succeeded him. But we have seen reason for thinking that Nudd served this purpose. At any rate he seems to have had the ordering of the Hounds of Hell. Since, however, Nudd and Ludd are apparently the same, and Ludd is the Irish Lugh, Nudd is also a god of Light. There is perhaps no distinction between the Lords of Light and Darkness at this stage and the Great Mother, the Lady of the Dark, has dropped out of the story. By one of those curious twists which are so commonly met with by students of old religions, the Christian Devil, the Lord of Darkness, became known as Lucifer and Beelzebub, both of whom were Lords of Light. This is the usual fate of the gods of one religion when it is mastered by another and can be used as a kind of rough gauge when studying the succession of beliefs. The gods of one stage become the demons of the next.

Chapter Seven

IF the reader has studied Professor E. O. James's *Prehistori*
Religion, he will have formed some idea of the huge area whicl
was once under the sway of the Great Mother belief. From Indi;
into Asia Minor, over most of the Mediterranean lands anc
right up to the Channel Islands innumerable objects have beer
found to testify to this belief. They range from thousands of littl
statuettes to menhirs with no more on them than an indication o
a pair of breasts. The cult goes far back in time before the Age o
Bronze. How far back it will be found to extend, nobody can tell
but it would not be an extravagant guess to say that the little
ivory female carvings found over much of Palaeolithic Europe
may belong to the same group of ideas. Right across the Atlantic
on the islands of the Caribbean, the little female statuettes are
found with polished stone axes, which remind one strongly o
similar objects from the eastern end of the Mediterranean. I
would not be an exaggeration to say that the belief in the Grea
Mother covered the whole of the ancient world, not everywhere
at the same time, of course, but at some stage of the develop
ment of man.

The worship of Diana, or Artemis, is a development of thi
Great Mother belief and this is at the root of the religion o
witches. One of the chief tests of the witch-hunters, as Dr
Murray tells us, was the presence of the bodies of supposec
witches of extra teats on which they were believed to feed theii
animal familiars. These teats of course had no real existence
they were non-malignant tumours of some kind, due to abnor
mal cell development of the body. But their existence wa
enough to condemn the unfortunate woman to the stake. There
are just as many of these growths on male bodies today, but the

witch-hunters appear to have ignored this fact. Now the origin of this particular idea is obvious. Artemis was the Great Mother of beast as well as man. Great numbers of statues representing Diana in this guise exist (Fig. 1 (b), p. 21). They are found, from time to time, from Asia Minor to Marseilles. They do not represent the Huntress Diana with her bow and deer; but Diana as the Great Mother. Here she is shown with the top half of her body entirely covered with superimposed rows of breasts. The lower half has a corresponding series of tiers of beasts of various kinds. Diana, as the Vangelo says, was Queen of Witches all! These beasts are her familiars. Whether the modern witches still have familiars I do not know; but isolated cases still existed, within twenty miles of Cambridge in this century, of women who were said by the villagers to have them. The witch was simply representing the Great Mother, the Artemis of the Ephesians.

The cult of the Great Mother was so long-lived and so wide-spread that it would be quite impossible to reduce it to a few chapters in a short book. Many peoples had different names for the deity and for every real name there were many epithets used to indicate which deity was being mentioned, without actually using the real name. As I said before, this was to prevent hostile magic being employed through the use of her name. It is possible also that many devotees were too frightened to use a word of such great power.

As we have seen before, the Great Mother cult was supplanted in time by the belief in a Greater Father. Whether this represents a true evolution in belief, like that from totemism to anthropomorphism, may be doubted. The pictures in the Palaeolithic caves suggest that the male totemistic shaman figure was at least as, and perhaps more, important in the ideas of the early hunting tribes as that of the female fertility figures indicated by small carvings. It was more important to hunters to get their game than to see its reproduction. It is probable that two conceptions existed, from very early times, side by side. In one the male element was predominant, in the other the female.

With the taming of animals, the female idea of Motherhood became increasingly important. The fertility of the stock was the vital need of the nomadic tribe. Unless their beasts increased in numbers, how could they eat them? They might milk them, of course, but they must eat something. The Great Mother must see to it. But the Father still hung about in the background. After all he had to help and who kept the wolves and lions off the stock?

As time went on nomads tended to become more anchored to certain areas. Grass was better in some places than others, all the year round. Nomads tended to settle down in these places. First they put a ring of stones round the bottom of their tent to keep it from flapping in the wind. Then they built a wall upon them to keep the wind out. Finally they made the whole thing into a permanent hut. As the men were out after their stock by day, the women slowly evolved a primitive culture of edible vegetable fruits. Little by little, by trial and error, agriculture became first a support to stock-breeding, and then of greater importance. Agriculture was for many centuries the woman's business. Not only was she the cook and the support of the man, she became the boss. It was natural therefore for Great Mother belief to dominate the religious ideas of the early villager and then the primitive townsman. But town never ousted country. Nomads might be getting fewer; but hunting tribes still exist today.

In the lands where woman's rule became predominant, descent was through the mother. The chieftainess, or queen, was all-important as long as she was capable of breeding, and even afterwards as the power to knock her daughter over the head with a rolling-pin if she did not behave. She probably became the intermediary with the Great Mother; the gnarled old priestess, whose word was law. But the queen was the earthly representative of the Great One, the living symbol of fertility, as long as her powers of child-bearing lasted. She had to be fertile, or nothing would be fertile. If she were not, the Great Mother must have turned away her face and disaster threatened the tribe. Therefore the queen had to have a mate to make her fertile. Much has been written on this question by many authorities, but Sir James Fraser and Charles Graves are the names which are most closely associated with it.

The usual plan seems to have been for the queen to have a mate for a limited time. This might be for a year, or for seven years. After this time had elapsed, a new mate was chosen and the old one usually was dispatched in a more or less brutal manner. It is not for nothing that such goddesses as Durga and Kali in India and Black Annis in England were blood-thirsty monsters.

Now men, however attractive the queens may have been and however much they enjoyed royal authority over the other men of the tribe, have a rooted objection to being murdered in a revolting manner to make way for a rival. Even the idea that their mangled bodies would fertilize the land can have had but little appeal. But custom is strong. I do not think matriarchal society broke up easily. All through long ages people were torn to pieces yearly to satisfy a religious belief, which seems completely absurd to us. It takes a praying mantis to enjoy this kind of thing. Even spiders have found a way out of the difficulty.

I think matriarchy was overthrown by war. This was not a war between men and Amazons; although this classical myth may retain traces of some such happening. I fancy it came about through the worship of dead heroes. The queen's mate had of necessity to be head of the young tribal warriors. As long as weapons were of a Stone Age kind and fighting was mostly a matter of shooting with weak bows and throwing stone- or bone-tipped spears, casualties were not heavy and the hero had little chance to show what he could really do. But when efficient cutting weapons, particularly cutting swords, evolved in the Bronze Age, war took on a more serious aspect. The fort was made to stop the enemy getting to close quarters and the enemy stormed it. Now the man who led the attack on the wall, or the fellow who stood on the wall and beat off the rush by his determined bravery, began to assume greater stature than the woman, who only bore children and waited anxiously in her hut for her throat to be cut, if the defence gave way. The dead hero, who had never been beaten, became something worth remembering. Men saw, or thought they saw, his figure fighting beside them. Then men began to murmur, 'Who beat off those stinking swine?' 'We did and old so-and-so was there to help us. I saw him.' 'So did I.' Little by little old so-and-so became a god. To the deeds he had done became added those of many dead warriors before and after his lifetime. In this way the great Aryan god, Indra, was evolved. When the Aryans had overrun, conquered and settled much of India, this great hero, of a distant past and different land, married the Great Mothers of the conquered Dravidian peoples, Durga and Kali. They had not kept the Aryans out; Indra was too strong for them. They took second place. Indian mythology is obviously very confused for these goddesses were also wives of Siva.

However the change-over was slow in coming and sporadic in distribution. Unconquered peoples retained their matriarchy long after others had gone over to the rule of men and the worship of a Greater Father together with a Great Mother. Some peoples, especially in Africa, still killed their kings after set periods of rule, simply because the king had had to take over the function of ensuring fertility to the tribe. This was a stage at which, if Margaret Murray is right, the Normans had arrived at the time of William Rufus. How the Normans, a tough, vigorous, warlike people from the north, had become infected with a disease which was clearly not common in their homeland, is not easy to explain. They must have caught it in Normandy itself. I cannot recall anything in the Sagas to suggest that chiefs or kings were murdered for religious reasons, except in times very long before the Norman Conquest of England.

In Britain, in England of today, the change was apparently taking place at the time of the Roman Conquest. Two recorded stories seem to show this clearly. The first is that of Boadicea (Boudicca), queen of the Iceni; the second that of Cartimandua, queen of the Brigantes. I have mentioned this before in some other book, but will do so again, for I find it takes about twenty years before people believe anything I say. It does not matter how reasonable or unreasonable the matter is. It is simply a question of inertia and the difficulty people experience in grasping anything that they had not been taught before. The dead weight of the mass of information crammed into the heads of students to enable them to pass exams makes their minds far less flexible than those of people who have not had to suffer under this system. Some years ago I sent a copy of some papers I had written to a friend in America, who was interested in the subject. He replied thanking me and added that he would never have thought of my answer; but then, unlike him, I had never had to endure the tedium of taking a doctorate. I should hate to be known as 'doctor' and be called upon suddenly to deliver a baby in a railway carriage, or a bus, with no more qualification for the job than a doctorate of philosophy! But I must end this unwarranted digression and return to Boadicea (I dislike the correct name, Boudicca) and Cartimandua.

Boadicea, so Tacitus tells us, was queen of the Iceni. The Iceni at that time were a great tribe. Before the new cut in the Fens was made to let the Ouse out past Denver Sluice to King's Lynn and so isolated them from easy access to the northward, their territory appears to have included all Norfolk, Suffolk, part of Cambridgeshire and even, as the old name of Boston seems to show, part of Lincolnshire. They were an old Iron Age people and not Belgae, who, as Caesar tells us, had begun to settle southern Britain about a generation before his time in Gaul and visits to Britain. That is the Iceni were settled in eastern England long before the birth of Christ. They were an old Celtic people and their name was once, I think, 'Eachanaidh', the people of the Horse. Before the invasions of the Belgae, I fancy their lands extended right down the Chiltern ridge and over the Upper Thames. The Icknield Way is named after them. Owing to the pressure from the Belgae, they were squeezed into a smaller area and a section of the tribe seems to have been compelled to migrate into western Scotland, where they became known to the Roman geographer Ptolemy as the Epidii, from the Gaulish 'epos' and Greek 'ippos', a horse. There they are still known in Knapdale, Kintyre and the islands as MacEacherns, the sons of the Horse. There some of them still retain vague memories of being connected with horses in some supernatural way. The difference between Iceni and MacEacherns on the one hand and Epidii on the other is only the difference between the Gaelic and Welsh forms of the Celtic speech.

In about the year A.D. 61, after the conquest of southern England by the armies of the Emperor Claudius, the king of the Iceni, Prasutagus, died, leaving, so the Romans affirmed, part of his kingdom to them. Tacitus tells how officials went to extract their portion of the legacy and in the process scourged Boadicea and violated her daughters. Instantly the Iceni rose in arms and in a furious campaign wrought more trouble to Rome than it had ever experienced in Britain. Colchester, St. Albans and London were all stormed and sacked. Great numbers of female captives were sacrificed by Boadicea to Andrastea; apparently Adrasteia, who was a somewhat indefinite character in classical mythology, but a moon goddess in Egypt. We are not concerned here with the defeat of Boadicea and the ravaging of eastern Britain; but we are concerned with the causes of the revolt. It seems perfectly clear that Prasutagus had no right to will away the territory, or anything else, because he was only king by right of being the husband of the queen. The Romans, it seems, had not understood this and had committed the greatest sacrilege in scourging the living representative of the Great Mother and forcibly putting themselves in the position of mates to the daughters by whom the sacred line descended. Or they may have understood perfectly well and have done it to show that matriarchy was ended. They had made a trifling mistake if this were the case; it was not ended in the north for a thousand years.

The case of Cartimandua also involved the Romans in wars. She was queen of the Brigantes, who were also a pre-Belgic tribe. They seem to have occupied most of the country from Humber to Cheviot. Cartimandua was a friend of Rome, or more probably an enemy of the Belgae. In A.D. 51, when the Belgic hero, Caratacus, was finally defeated by the Romans, after being driven out of southern Britain and making a long stand in the Welsh mountains, he fled to Cartimandua for protection. He did not seek protection from the king, whose name was Venutius, but from the head of the tribe. At least that is the interpretation I put on the incident. The queen handed him over to the Romans. No doubt they were gratified by the present of a man who had been as elusive and dangerous as Owen Glendour was to prove in a later age. Some time later, Cartimandua wished to change her husband for his standard-bearer. This was probably no more than the accepted matriarchal custom, but Venutius was 'a master of war'. Cartimandua evidently was unable to sway the tribe against him. She appealed to the Romans for help. They sent a force to rescue her and she fades from the picture. The war, however, remained with Rome and it proved a long and painful business.

Now the Brigantes were the people of Brigid, who was a Great Mother goddess venerated not only in England, but in Ireland also. She was so important that she could not be displaced and, under Pope Gregory's dictum, she became a saint. She remains one of the most revered saints in Ireland today. In the case of the Brigantes and Cartimandua we appear to see the change from matriarchy to patriarchy not only taking place, as in the example of Boadicea and the Iceni, but almost completed

Had Rome not intervened, Venutius would have remained king. No doubt there would have been uprisings in support of legitimist candidates who had married into the royal female line, for this happened in Scotland. Centuries after a patriarchal Scottish king had, by marriage to a Pictish princess, introduced male descent into a matriarchal country, husbands of the legitimate female heir to the throne fought in attempts to establish their claim to it. I think I wronged Cartimandua in another book, *The Painted Men*, by saying she was a licentious woman. According to her religious upbringing she was no doubt entirely respectable. She was the living representative of the Great Mother and was required to change her husband at the appropriate time. Venutius had probably completed his correct term of office, which in Ireland appears to have been seven years, and it was time for him to make way for a younger man. Presumably he did not fancy whatever was the traditional termination of his career among the Brigantes; and the tribe itself, in troublous times, preferred to have a master of war at their head, rather than a less experienced tactician, however efficient he may have been in the production of royal children. I must say I rather hope it was the standard-bearer's head that Sir Mortimer Wheeler found at the bottom of the ditch of Venutius's stronghold. Venutius may have been a bit of a 'blimp', as the enormous extent of his fortifications at Stanwick seems to suggest, but at least he did not hand over a gallant soldier to the enemy.

In southern Britain then, Great Mothers were going out of fashion soon after the beginning of the Christian era. In Ireland they remained, in folk belief at any rate, long enough for tales about them to be written down by Christian monks. Some districts probably retained the worship until the conversion of the land to Christianity. But no religion is accepted everywhere at the same time. Pockets of believers survive here and there and hand their religion on generation after generation. Sometimes indeed the pendulum swings once more and the supplanted belief returns. This has happened more than once with the devotion to the Great Mother, but never again did it re-establish the matriarchal system.

I think there was only one Great Mother and it is her local names and epithets which cause confusion. We are dealing with such a great length of time, at least four thousand years, and with such wide diffusion of peoples, that of course there are many names. The essential belief, spreading probably from only one centre, was quite simple. There was one Great Mother of All, she had made everything that lived and grew, she was at first both Darkness and Light. Then she divided off Light into a separate personality and made him her husband, but he was in no sense her equal. He might be the Sun and give off more light and heat, but she was the fount of life and chose only to show herself dimly as the Moon. Things grew mysteriously in the night, for she made them grow. The love-making took place in the moonlight, or in the dark. It was not often that children or animals were born in the day-time, but in the hours when the Great Mother held her sway. Without her influence nothing was born and nothing grew. In her hours of rule old people died. She was both destroyer and creator. This I think was the whole of the original belief; everything else was just trappings. Of course she gave success in love, for fertility was her business; and woman, as her representative, had to be importuned, as she herself had to be importuned. The moon grew from the dark, swelled to full size and then dwindled away again; so did mankind. Thus, as Robert Graves has demonstrated in his *Greek Myths* and other works, the Great Mother came to be regarded as having three aspects, the New Moon, the Full Moon and the Waning Moon. So there were three aspects of the Great Mother and she appears to us, if we do not know this fact, as three distinct goddesses. Each of these goddesses has a different name and many different epithets in every area where she was worshipped. Where tribes have mingled, either by conquest or in other ways, the numbers of goddesses increase, three at each mixing of the population. Each of these has the attributes given to her by her original tribe. Yet all these goddesses are really only one. The more frequent the conquests of a given area, the more complicated become its gods, until something drastic comes along like Christianity or Mohammedanism and sweeps the whole lot into the limbo, where they remain as sad ghosts in folk memory. Therefore our study cannot possibly be easy, or clear-cut. We are really only scratching about in a forgotten midden for neglected scraps. Proof of anything must be almost impossible to obtain. Even when the representation of a god or goddess comes to light anywhere, except in a classical setting, there are usually as many opinions as to what it represents as there are experts on that particular period.

In the Roman provinces of Gaul and Britain there was a development from the three aspects of the Great Mother and she became three Mothers. Presumably this was the result of a misunderstanding of the original idea; but, however it came about, statues of the three Matronae are quite commonly found. In Mrs. Brogan's *Roman Gaul* we are told that they survive today in France as three fairies.

In Britain, however, a much greater complication appears to have occurred, for since the Great Mother had three aspects and three apparent personalities, if there were three Great Mothers all of one aspect, they must obviously have each possessed two other aspects, or personalities. You then get nine goddesses out of one. This is probably the origin of the frequent occurrence of Nine Maidens, particularly in connection with the names of sacred springs. In Scotland in particular these maidens are often associated with Brigid. There were probably no other maidens originally, save Brigid alone. It is interesting to note that the Teutonic goddess of war became nine Valkyries.

A friend of mine, who has now been dead a long time, the late Mansfield Forbes of Clare College, Cambridge, was fascinated by these Nine Maidens and hunted for them all over the country. His friends believed that he made a habit of driving up to country houses, ringing the bell, and asking whoever came out if they had any Nine Maidens in the neighbourhood. As he habitually wore spectacles mended with sealing-wax and pipe-cleaners and was often clad in a tattered kilt and not much else, it is remarkable that he was never arrested as a dangerous vagabond. I do not think that he ever published his results and am doubtful whether they would help us much if he had; but the Nine Maidens and their association, not only with Brigid, but with a dragon, are certainly part of our Great Mother picture. The dragon may well be the same old beast who was cast out by Michael and worsted by Indra.

I once went with Manny Forbes on his quest for Nine Maidens. This was not a long business, but a simple visit to some springs, known as 'Nine Wells', at Whittlesford, a few miles from Cambridge. There were not nine wells, only a few water-holes in a large field. Manny expressed his determination to perform some

83

kind of ritual ablution in them. Layard, the psychologist, who was one of the party, hastily remarked, 'All right, Manny, but are you quite sure you want to have a baby?' The preparations for the ritual were instantly abandoned.

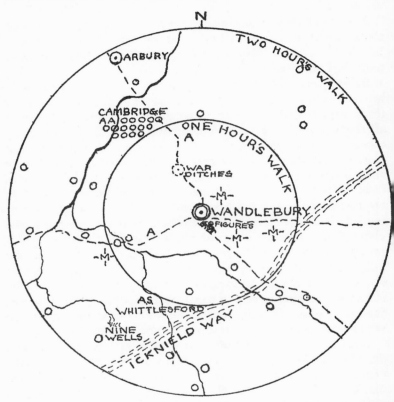

Fig. 9. Sketch map of the country within a six-mile radius of Wandlebury. Other groups of Andrew dedications are found outside this area and appear to be related to important Romano-British sites. A = Church with dedication to Andrew; S = Shiela-na-gig; M = Mag's, Meg's or Maggot's Hill; O = Church with no significant dedication; ⊙ = Iron Age Fort; - - - = Presumed Iron Age Trackway.

This rather ridiculous incident serves as an introduction to a district full of traces of the ancient gods. Close beside Nine Wells there used to be a group of barrows. These were destroyed long ago, but are described in Sir Cyril Fox's *Archaeology of the Cambridge Region*. Each barrow contained an important Iron Age burial in a large box tomb, of the type I excavated at Snailwell some years ago and described in *The Painted Men*.

Nine Wells then was obviously near to the home of an important Iron Age family. Four such localities within a circle of fifteen miles radius—the Bartlow Hills, Lord's Bridge, Snailwell and Nine Wells—are all valley sites and close to water. They were evidently the homes of chieftains, or duinwassails, in the age when the continental civilization of Rome had begun to creep over the country, but before the British had become completely romanized. Nine Wells is not within our 'hour's walk' distance of Wandlebury Camp, the only really important Iron Age stronghold for many miles, but it is less than two, and the three-mile circle is quite arbitrary. The hour's walk circle round Wandlebury Camp contains more traces of the old gods than any area I have yet examined; but it is improbable that it is unusual in this respect. A careful collection of information round about other obvious Iron Age sites would almost certainly produce similar results all over the country. Moreover the information has largely been written down already and it is only a question of collecting it round a focus. There is no need for extensive training in archaeology, nor for expensive excavation, the material is available, in libraries or tithe maps, for anyone who has the time and enthusiasm to look for it.

Over the low hill to the east of Nine Wells lies the church of St. Mary at Whittlesford. Over the south doorway, in the side of the tower, is a round-headed Norman, or possibly late Saxon, window. The head of the window consists of a single irregular stone, carved on the face of it with the figure of a naked woman, sitting facing the observer in an indelicate posture. Over her leans a nude male figure, with moustache and beard (Fig. 10). Such female figures are known as Shiela-na-gigs and are quite common on churches. But it is rare to find a male figure associated with the female. The Whittlesford carving clearly represents the Great Mother and her mate, Baal, Lucifer, or whatever he happened to be called.

Although these Shiela-na-gigs appear most indecent to modern eyes, it is clear that they did not do so to churchmen of the Middle Ages. They come from priories and nunneries as well as from parish churches. Some of them are not ancient stones which had to be included owing to the veneration paid to them by the villagers. They were cut to be included in the design of the church. No one could pretend that the Whittlesford object was not intended to be seen. The stone was cut to fit the window and its position is such that one feels some qualms when standing outside the church to look at it. The only real explanation seems to be that both old and new beliefs were mingled together in the minds, not only of the parishioners, but of the clergy themselves. This is borne out by Margaret Murray's works, in which she gives instances of both priests and bishops being censured, but not severely punished, for taking part in fertility ritual. I have already mentioned the case of the monks at Frithelstock in Devon, who were found by the bishop of Exeter venerating a statue resembling Diana. The remarkable thing about all this is, not so much that it existed, for similar overlap is to be found in India, where the high beliefs in Brahma combine with the more primitive fertility cults of Siva and Mahadevi;

a.

b.

Fig. 10. Two Shiela-na-gigs.

(a) Above the south door of Whittlesford church, carved to form the head of a Norman window.

(b) Believed to have been on the wall of a priory building at St. Ives, Hunts, built about A.D. 1008 and destroyed by fire in A.D. 1207. The stone is burnt (after H. J. M. Green).

but that almost all the datable evidence points to a time later than the Norman Conquest for its prevalence in England. The replacement of the Anglo-Saxon kings and their supplanting by

Frenchmen, who were devotees of the witch cult, appears to have encouraged a revival of popular beliefs which were at least hidden in Anglo-Saxon times. Attempts have been made to blame the Norsemen for this revival; but this seems to be wrong. There is little evidence for Mother Goddesses in the Sagas; although there may be a little which points to the veneration of the reproductive powers of the stallion. In fact it seems more probable that fertility beliefs were introduced from the British Isles, or France, into the North at about the same time that William established his rule in England. William, as we have already seen, was the son of Robert the Devil and father of William Rufus, who is thought to have been sacrificed in accordance with the old pagan ritual.

It seems clear that, if the Mother Goddess could not be driven out of popular belief at the conversion to Christianity, the Gregorian instruction would have applied to her as well as to her consorts. We have already seen that Brigid has become St. Brigid. In other parts of the country, the obvious candidate was the actual Mother of Christ. Dedications to St. Mary are, however, so numerous that it seems hardly worth while to examine them like Michael and Andrew. It is interesting, however, to note that Whittlesford church is in fact dedicated to St. Mary and St. Andrew. The remains of a large alabaster carving of a crowned female figure with bared breasts is still preserved in the church. Whether this figure represented the Madonna, or St. Catherine, there seems little doubt that it would have been viewed as the Great Mother by those parishioners who were still that way inclined. The patron saints, according to what we have already learnt, would seem to be the Great Mother and Mabon; that is, symbolically the Moon and Sun.

The whole question of Shiela-na-gigs is somewhat confused by their name. The sole authority for its use comes from an English-speaking gentleman in Ireland, who asked an old countryman what one of the figures was. The old man was thought to say that it was a Shiela-na-gig. This term as it stands is difficult to translate. Remembering that Erse was a dying language, being steadily ousted by 'quaint English' for a long time, and that some enquirers are a little hard of hearing, we may well wonder whether Shiela-na-gig is the correct term at all. Some people have translated it as 'the lady of the castle' and others 'the lady

87

of the breasts'. Since the real name of a goddess must not be mentioned by believers, it is probable that the old man only used an epithet. The first word is not difficult; if it is not simply a girl's name, Shiela, and referring to some notorious character in the neighbourhood, it seems probable that the word was Sithlach (pronounced Shiela) and meant 'Holy Lady'. 'Na' simply means 'of the'. So we have 'Holy Lady of the', but what is 'Gig'? Supposing it was 'breast', the word would have been 'cioche', pronounced something like 'keesh'. Margaret Murray has pointed out that many Shiela-na-gigs have hardly any breasts at all. The emphasis is on other parts of their anatomy. In any case 'keesh' would hardly become 'gig' in any language. 'Castle' seems equally improbable. It seems to me that 'gig' is simply a form of 'Gog', of 'og', 'ug' and perhaps 'hog'. It appears to be a variant of God. If this is the right explanation, the old man was really giving a correct description. The figure represented 'the holy lady of the god'; she was a Mother Goddess. She sits in the attitude of Baubo, in the Mediterranean countries in classical times, to emphasize this side of her activities. Baubo of the Mediterranean is the Badb of ancient Ireland. At Wandlebury and presumably Whittlesford, she was Ma Gog, the Mother Goddess.

Ma Gog's hills, representing her breasts, like the Cailleach's paps on Jura and the breasts of Danu in Ireland, surround Wandlebury within our hour's walk circle. There are three of them today, but a fourth has recently been canonized and has lapsed from Magg's or Megg's Hill to that of St. Margaret. They are all rounded, mammiform hills and there are no others with that name for miles in every direction. This canonizing of places is a nuisance and used to cause great annoyance to that fine old Cambridgeshire antiquary, W. M. Palmer. He was furious to find that the village of Papworth Agnes had suddenly become Papworth St. Agnes. 'What do they want to do that for?' he exclaimed. 'Don't they know that Agnes was a king's mistress?' I forget which king it was, one of the Edwards I fancy, but I could sympathize with my old friend's indignation. This kind of smug improving of time-honoured names is a public nuisance. If Dr. Palmer had not been an indefatigable research worker in his own area, nobody would have guessed the true origin of the name. I hope someone will show the fellow who has turned Magog's breast into St. Margaret's Hill, after two thousand years of popular regard, what a tiresome, interfering rascal he is. It does not take long to change a whole countryside. When I first worked at Cambridge there were two villages side by side above the plain, Chishill and Crishill. Then one day one of them appeared with a 'hall' in place of a 'hill'. 'Why have you changed the name of your village?' I asked one of the inhabitants. 'Oh, the parson wanted it,' he replied. Somebody investigating the sites of old halls may well be taken in by this.

Let us, however, return to Magog and not fume about the desecration of her anatomy. The hills on which Wandlebury stands are known to many thousands of Cambridge people as the Gogs or Gogmagogs. The old countrymen call them Gogamagogs and, although I have never heard of it, I am told that not long ago they called them Hoggogamagog hills. In a recent book called *Gogmagog*, I described the legend relating to this place and the folk-lore connected with it, which led to the search for a hill-cut giant on the slope facing Whittlesford and the apparent discovery of three. These figures, one of which has now been excavated Fig. 2(b), are apparently those of two males and one female with a horse.

Attempts have been made to show that the figures were made by glacial conditions in the Ice Age, but these attempts explain nothing and need not concern us here. I think that one of the figures is the rising sun, another the moon and the third Wandil, a demon, who has given his name to Wandlebury. The other two are Magog and Gog. Magog, according to such authorities as Sir Cyril Fox, is earlier than the other two figures, which were probably added in the Roman period. Magog seems certainly to have been made by the builders of the great camp itself. She is a real Iron Age figure comparable to certain small Danish and Near Eastern antiquities and perhaps dating to about 200 B.C. (Fig. 11). Although the drawing of the original group of Magog and her horse is barbaric, yet it shows a sense of balance and forms a complete picture where it has not been damaged by a later trackway down the side of the hill (Fig. 12).

For some reason no one had ever thought that a goddess might appear on the hillside. There are two great male figures still to be seen at Cerne Abbas and Wilmington in the south of

England, while others are known to have vanished from Plymouth and Oxford in comparatively recent times. A female figure was, however, unknown and uncontemplated. Yet we should have thought of it, for Irish story is full of great goddesses

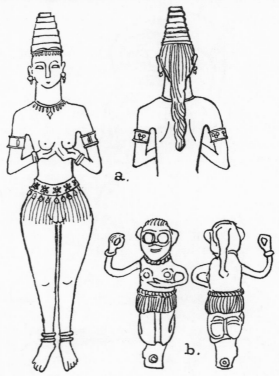

Fig. 11.

(a) Sketch from a painting by James Mellaart of an electrum figure of a goddess found at Dorak and believed to date about 2500 B.C. The hair style and string skirt are similar to those of the Faardal figurine (b). (After Hans Kjaer.)

and tales of them survive in both English and Scottish folk-lore. Archaeologists, however, are largely governed by what they can see and handle. The idea had grown up that hill figures were always men, or horses; a female figure was abominable. Well, there she is with her horse and three years of work went into her uncovering. She had been renovated apparently at the time the other two figures were cut and fresh chalk was put into her outlines where they had become brown and discoloured by weathering. This renovation, which incidentally covered evidence that

Fig. 12. Wandlebury Goddess separated from her mount. Missing portions dotted in. Compare hairstyle and position of hand with figurines from Faardal and Dorak (Fig. 11).

her outlines had been exposed when climate was much the same as now, altered some of her original appearance. When we cleared her out it became plain that she was an Artemis with several breasts, probably four. She points to them with her right hand. In the left, like Brigid, she holds a disc, which is probably

91

intended to represent the 'Apple of Life' (Fig. 12). Above her head, a great horned shape has not been excavated, but is probably a moon symbol. The association with the horse is most important, for not only is the horse what we might have expected, if the builders of Wandlebury were Iceni, the horse folk; but the horse is a symbol of the sun. It seems that the picture as a whole is intended to suggest that the sun is about to mate with the moon. Lucifer and Diana are shown here in very primitive guise. This hippogamous, if we may call it so, idea is not confined to Britain. Giraldus Cambrensis, when writing his twelfth-century account of Ireland, describes in shocked terms the induction of a king of Donegal. Although he does not more than hint at the actual mating, it is clear that the king had to behave as a stallion, going on all fours, and then, when the grey mare had been sacrificed, bathe in broth made from the carcass, drink it and eat the flesh. He was being turned into a stallion by magical rites. Since the Fir Domnan, his people, were patriarchal, the rite was performed in the reverse way. In India, however, the warrior caste, the Kshatriyas, had a ceremony at the first horse sacrifice after a great rajah's accession which seems to correspond exactly with the ideas suggested by the Wandlebury figure. At the asvamheda, as it was called, the rajah's wife had to go through a ceremony of semi-mating with a sacred stallion, which was afterwards killed. Here at such different places, thousands of miles apart, we are evidently once again at the edge of a ring of thought. The idea had started from one centre and ended up in the north of Ireland and the plains of India. It is clearly a thing dating from the change-over from totemism to anthropomorphism and explains the many examples in Greek myth of gods changing into stallions to secure women they desired. Epona, a great Gaulish goddess, was believed to have been fathered by a man on a mare (Fig. 2 (a), p. 33). No one has explained satisfactorily as yet why the supposed leaders of the Anglo-Saxon invaders in the fifth century of our era should have been known as Hengist and Horsa, for 'hengst' means a horse and 'horsa' a mare. It is reasonably certain that their invasion did not take place in the way it is described in the Anglo-Saxon Chronicle and it seems probable that these two mythical heroes were in reality religious conceptions.

There are several variants of the story of Hengist and Horsa.

Many scholars now believe that the whole episode really belongs to the Iron Age before the Roman Conquest of Britain and that it was deliberately altered to fit into the Anglo-Saxon Chronicle and the histories of Nennius and Geoffrey of Monmouth. The early part of the Chronicle is certainly not a true account and items appear to have been interpolated which did not even take place in Britain, but in Ireland. Historical fact does not really appear in the Chronicle before the middle of the sixth century, when the campaigns of Ceawlin have the ring of truth. It seems quite possible then that the dealings of Vortigern with Hengist and Horsa are garbled stories of what happened at the time of the Belgic invasions, either of Britain or even of Ireland. The point, however, which interests us here is the account of the marriage between the Celtic king, Vortigern, and Rowen, the daughter of Hengist, the horse. This looks very like another case of hippo-gamy. Rowen is a name of Welsh type.

The whole of this hippogamous idea must be of immense age, dating perhaps from a time when the horse had been domesti-cated only recently; but a man disguised as a horse still appears in the witch trials of the sixteenth century, mating with the women of the coven. These strange beliefs had an enormous length of life. There is on the wall of the Royston Cave, that curious underground artificial cavern in the chalk, amid large numbers of carvings of a religious character dating from about the fourteenth century, a group representing a stallion, Shiela-na-gig, sun-disc and sword, which apparently show at least a remembrance of the ritual.

I do not think that the hill figures at Wandlebury, or any-where else, were intended to be worshipped of themselves. They were, I think, used for a ceremony, which re-enacted some impor-tant scene in the life of the gods. They were more in the nature of a stage than of an image. But in whatever manner they were employed, it seems evident that the old religion was very strongly centred close to Cambridge. It is at least curious that there is known to have been another giant at Oxford. Whether quite so many traces remain there as round Wandlebury can, I feel, be left to Oxford itself to find out; but I do know that there was once a Shiela-na-gig on an Oxford church and the name Horsepath is found by the hill where the giant was known to exist before the great Civil War.

There are so many pointers to the importance of the Wandle-bury area in old religious custom that it may well serve as a type of what to look for in other districts. First there is a legend of three figures and a horse; then there are folk tales of yesterday relating to three giants and a horse. When we find the figures, one is a Mother Goddess with a stallion. Next the two nearest churches are dedicated to St. Andrew, who is thought to have been the god Mabon, the young sun. The rising sun appears to be associated with the moon above the Mother Goddess on the hillside. At Whittlesford, within about the correct distance, the church is dedicated to St. Mary and St. Andrew, who are thought to be the Mother Goddess and Mabon respectively. On the church tower is a carving, which apparently represents the Holy Lady of the god, together with the god himself. There are four hills, which seem to have been named after the Mother God-dess's breasts, and when we came to excavate that Mother Goddess's figure on the hill, she had three or four breasts. Finally there is Nine Wells, which in other districts appears to be associated with the Great Mother, Brigid. Our Great Mother figure seems to have Brigid's attribute, the apple of life, in her left hand. If you remove any couple of these items, you are still left with too many for coincidence. The epithet for the goddess still clings to the countryside, after the invasions of Roman, Saxon, Viking and Norman have rolled over it. How much more must remain in other places less troubled by war and immigration.

One other point remains before we leave this eastern area. Twenty years or more ago, Professor F. Heichelheim, now of Toronto, drew our attention in Cambridge to the unusual num-ber of little statuettes of Hercules of Roman date found in the area. Hercules, as we have seen, is one of the aspects in which Baal was portrayed and that borne not only by the Dagda, the Mother Goddess Macha's wife in Ireland, but by the great figure of the Cerne Giant in Dorset. Macha, the lady of the plain, is surely our Ma Gog and the Hercules figures are meant to represent Dagda, who in the former Marshland territory of the Iceni was known as Hiccafrith (trust of the Iceni).

Slowly, but it seems surely, as we pick up our clues and bring them together, they begin to form a net, and when it is at last pulled tight and drawn up on the beach, it will be found to con-tain quite a lot of fishes. These fishes could never have been caught by using a single line and hook, whether it was an archaeological line, anthropological, folk-lore or any other. For this kind of study we need any kind of line we can lay hands on and as many of them as possible. This is not a popular way of doing things today, but it is the only way to do it.

The specialist for instance may identify large numbers of Hercules figurines made in the same workshop. He may know the date within a few years. He may know all the classical information there is about the god portrayed by these little figures. If, however, he knows nothing about Hiccafrith, whose story comes from folk-lore, he is limited to saying that there must have been a cult of Hercules somewhere in the area. But Hiccafrith is still remembered and talked about. His grave is still shown. He is a Hercules figure, with a wagon-pole for a club and a wheel, a sun symbol, as a shield. He is the trust of the Hiccas, the Iceni. Furthermore he is a stone-throwing giant. His stones went through church walls. He is therefore hostile to the Christian faith. Then we pull the line of witch-cult study. Diana had a lover, Lucifer. Lucifer is a sun god. Beelzebub is a sun god, Baal. Baal, turning to historical study, was portrayed as a giant figure with a club. Hiccafrith then is a kind of Baal. The Hiccafrith grave is an enclosure in Marshland, which belonged to the Iceni. It was probably their summer grazing land. Hiccafrith becomes the Sun husband of the Icenean moon and horse goddess, Ma Gog. We get Magog from place names and we see what she was like by archaeology. In this way the former religion of the Iceni grows before our eyes. There may be mistakes in building up the picture, but it makes sense and conforms to the information available. As the work progresses we shall be able to add to it.

Now let us look at Magog again. The name, I fancy, means no more than Ma God, Mother God, the Great Mother, while Dagda is just Daddad, the Great Father. In India there is Mahadevi, wife along with Durga, Kali, Purvati and others of Siva. Siva is, I think, a Balor, Baal, Belinus and so on with a Burning eye. He burnt off one of Brahma's five heads. Siva is worshipped in many simple Indian homes as the lingam, the phallus, the male principle, Mahadevi as the yoni, or female principle. They are thus, on this level of thought, for they have higher attributes, the Great Father and Great Mother. But Siva is also the great destroyer of life, and of his wives, Durga and Kali are especially murderous. Mahadevi appears to mean something like Great Holy Mother and is presumably the Great Mother in a more benign aspect than Kali and Durga. Nevertheless she is probably the same goddess in origin. In Irish story we have very much the same thing and the clue is given to us there. The Badb, one of the great goddesses, is made to say that she has more than thirty-one names. This is tantamount to saying that she is all of the names we know. Brigid, Macha, Morrigan, Graney, Danu, the Cailleach are just variants of the Badb. Macha, who comes closest in name to Ma Gog, is an epithet. Magh, or Machair, is a fertile plain. Macha is a great Earth goddess; but she is also Dagda's wife and the wife of a Druid, who is obviously a later addition. One of the myths of Macha involves her in a race against horses when she was pregnant. She wins the race, but gives birth to a child and dies, cursing the men of Ulster with the pangs of childbirth in times of crisis. Macha is linked then with horses and childbirth, corresponding, it seems, to Ma Gog in this respect. Mahadevi is not, as far as I know, linked with horses, but she is linked with female fertility. It may be Mahadevi who was represented by the rajah's wife at the Asvamheda ceremony.

Kali and the Cailleach, whose name is variously pronounced Calyick, Calyuck or Colyuck, have much in common. The Scottish version of Cailleach, as recorded in folk tales, is nearer to the Indian Kali than the more sophisticated version found in the old Irish literature. Both the Indian and Scottish goddesses have black or blue-black faces and a monstrous eye in the middle of their foreheads. Kali has three eyes. In the Irish tale the Cailleach has beautiful eyes. Both are killers of men and portray the Great Mother in her old aspect. The Scottish Cailleach, in fact, keeps the youthful version of the goddess imprisoned in a cave on Ben Nevis, from whence she is rescued by Diarmid, the youthful sun god, the Scottish equivalent of Mabon. The English version of the Cailleach is Black Annis, who is also provided with the monstrous eye, is of a dark, unpleasant colour and murders men by dropping on them from a tree in the Dane Hills in Leicestershire. Black Annis is thus another Kali and her name, preserved as Annis, or Dane, is clearly the Danu, or Annu, of Ireland. Black Annis is still known in Yorkshire, where her curse is potent yet. Annis according to what we might perhaps term 'Gregory's law' became St. Ann. The Irish Cailleach apparently needed a new husband once in seven years. Nobody now knows the name of the husband of the Scottish Cailleach, but it may have been Manannan, lord of the sea. The Cailleach, the lady of the forest, carried a thunderbolt, raised foul weather and washed her dirty blanket in the whirlpool of Corrievreckan, between Scarba and Jura. On the lonely Jura shore of this gulf is the field of the Mare. On Jura itself are the Cailleach's Paps and on the opposite side of the strait in Knapdale a traditional story tells of attempts to pull her off her horse. This is the land of the Mac Eacherns, the Epidii, the People of the Horse.

As I have said before, the Epidii seem to have been a branch of the Iceni, pushed out of their homelands by the Belgic invasions. If one may make a reasoned guess, they had emigrated from the country round about the Uffington White Horse. In *Gogmagog* I gave reasons for thinking that the fine, or old lady, who rode on a white horse to Banbury Cross in the nursery rhyme was the same Cailleach and Lady Godiva was Gog diva, the holy lady of Gog, Magog. All these goddesses seem to me to be one and the same deity. The veiling of Godiva in her long hair seems to me to be an echo of the Gruagach, the fair-haired one of Western Scotland, who, as I have been assured, would appear out of the mist and lure young men to their deaths. In the Outer Islands, the Gruagach has now degenerated into a mischievous sprite, but this was not always the case; any more than Cailleach was always a term for any old woman. Anyone who has seen the Cailleach's breasts, two great hills on either side of Broadford in Skye, can hardly be mistaken on this point.

Black Annis was presumably the same as the Brigid whose people were the Brigantes. If this is correct, the Tuatha dé Danann, who were the people of the goddess Danu in Ireland, were of the same stock as the Brigantes. It is fashionable to speak of the Danann as consisting only of gods; but I am sure this is a mistake. They were a real people with a number of gods of whom Danu was the original. Like the witches in the Vangelo, Danu or Diana had made them skilled magicians and the tales connected with their magic have in the course of years transformed them all into gods. Precisely the same fate overtook the Fomori. This unknown people were once human beings, who

97

fought and traded in Scotland and Ireland. Today 'Fomor' is the Gaelic word for a giant and they have several rows of teeth. Story-telling was the great evening entertainment of the Celt and it is not surprising that continual embroidery of tales should have effected this transformation. Although the tales are made more attractive thereby, and some of the Irish tales like that of the Children of Lir are as beautiful as any in the world, it does not make it easy for anyone to sort them out and discover their original composition.

Quite a number of images of the old gods are now being

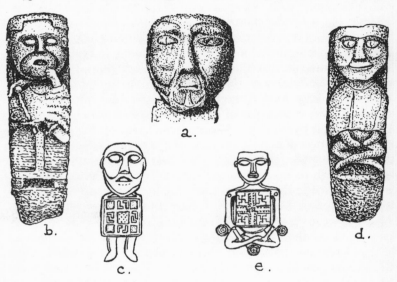

Fig. 13. Celtic gods from the British Isles.
    (a) Stone 'herm' from Corbridge identified as Mabon (after Ian Richmond).
    (b) Similar figure from White Island, Upper Loch Erne.
    (c) Irish bronze and enamelled figure of Mabon. Viking loot (after H. Shetelig).
    (d) Stone figure of Mother Goddess from White Island.
    (e) Bronze and enamelled Irish figure. Viking loot from the Oseberg ship-burial (Shetelig).
    Note Indian lotus, or yogi, position of d and e. Another figure from White Island has been identified by E. A. Armstrong as 'The Master of Animals'. A fourth is probably Ogmius.

identified in Britain and Ireland. The Sheila-na-gigs are quite common; but others sometimes masquerade as saints. Professor Ian Richmond identified two heads of Mabon from the Brigantian country south of the Roman Wall, which are published in *Dark Ages Britain*, edited by J. B. Harden (Fig. 13 (a)). These heads have hollows on the top for receiving offerings. A more spectacular group still exists on the site of an ancient chapel at White Island, Upper Lough Erne in Ireland (two are shown on Fig. 13). I have been involved in a minor controversy over these, for I could not bear to see them being described as St. Patrick and other holy men, when one of them was a lady wearing nothing but a lewd grin and a scanty cloak (Fig. 13 (d)). Five figures still are on view and it is thought that another lies buried near by. These figures, like Professor Richmond's Mabons, have hollows in their heads. The Rev. E. A. Armstrong, the learned author of *The Folklore of Birds*, has picked on one of the figures as being a deity known over much of the ancient world and usually shown with a pair of birds, perhaps we should call them a brace, in his hands. Unfortunately the name of this god is not known and it is difficult to equate him with any definite god of the Celtic world. Perhaps he is a kind of Pan; but we do not know enough to say anything definite. Here already, however, we have some unlikely companions for St. Patrick. One appears to be a Mother Goddess; the other a lord of nature. A third figure is plainly a warrior of some kind. It may be that he is the same god as that shown on the Devil's Stone at Copgrove (Fig. 4 (a)); but he has no horns and is not left-handed. This Celtic Mars could be either Teutates or Taramis if he had been found on the Continent. Here in Ireland, it is possible that he is a kind of Hero-god, perhaps Cuchulain. The carving clearly intends him to be young. The remaining two figures are meant to be older deities. The one apparently stroking his chin, wearing a sword and having a helmet on his head, must be surely a king of the gods (Fig. 13 (b)). He may be Nuada, holding up his silver hand, or Lugh himself. Lastly there is one with the open scroll on his knees. Is this a figure of Ogmius, who introduced writing? If it were so, one might have expected him to be holding something more like a tally stick on which oghams would be cut. This unique group shows at once the difficulty confronting anyone who tries to solve these problems. Opinions on what they represent differ so widely that they have been known both as the Seven Deadly Sins and St. Patrick and his converts. We cannot, however, get away from the figure with the birds, and the woman is not an unknown type. The date of the group is as uncertain as their names; but they are not earlier than the Roman period and probably not later than the eighth century. The kind of scabbard-end hanging below the war god's shield was common from late Roman times on into the seventh century. The penannular brooch that he wears could be as early as the first century, but continued in use for many centuries. It is perhaps more likely to be somewhere about the fifth century than either the first or the ninth. There is one other way of making an approximation and it leads to matters of considerable interest.

The cross-legged goddess is also found on an Irish bucket found in a Norwegian ship-burial (Fig. 13 (e)). This bucket must have come from Ireland, either as trade or loot, before the beginning of the ninth century, for it came from the burial of a Norwegian queen, who is confidently assumed to be Aasa who died in about A.D. 800. It was an old Celtic custom to put figures at the junction of the handle and the bucket and in Ireland it reached a high standard of workmanship. The seated figures on this Oseberg-ship bucket have cloaks covered with elaborate patterns in millefiori glass. Like the lady from Lough Erne, they wear nothing else. The resemblance might seem to be accidental, had not other Irish vessels been found in Viking graves, with figures which appear to represent different Celtic gods. One from Myklebostad is thought to have been buried in the ninth century. On it are three standing male figures, again with millefiori glass on their tunics, whose faces are made in the same style and by no means unlike that of the king at Lough Erne (Fig. 13 (ò)). There are also two separate examples of ornaments showing pairs of confronted human heads which apparently are attempts to display on a flat surface a double-headed, Janus-like god, who is found both in Gaul and Ireland.

In case it is thought that I am making too much of trivial objects, there is yet another bucket of Irish origin, which was found at Hexham in Northumberland close to the wall of the church. It contained more than eight thousand coins, thought to have been hidden about A.D. 867. The handles of this bucket have female figures supporting them, of which only the faces and breasts are clearly defined. These certainly suggest representations of the Great Mother. The reason for this is not hard to see. The buckets and pans were intended for foodstuffs, which might go bad. Figures of the Great Mother and other gods were put on the vessels as protective charms to preserve their contents.

The placing of charms on vessels used for storage of food, especially milk, is very widespread and is also of very great age. We could probably find cases of their employment today in every country of western Europe. Often they are simply drawn with the finger; but at times they became a kind of rash found on all pottery. Since the employment of any magic was pagan in character, there were ages when none could be employed openly. At others, when the rule of the Church was weakened, they appeared once more and it is interesting to see that when they did so, they were not new ideas, but ones of great antiquity. In Roman times the face of a goddess, unidentifiable, but probably the same Great Mother, is often found on jugs. I have found specimens myself. But on other vessels there is often a male face, which one sees described in serious reports as a 'rustic deity'. These things almost vanish with the termination of Roman rule; although the Germans often made breasts on their pots, both on the Continent and in England. These might not be recognized as such, if specimens were not sometimes found with the human face as well. With the coming of Christianity, all this fades from sight and remains underground for a very long time. It had not gone. People still carried out old rituals whether it was seeing the summer in with a certain amount of licence on May Eve, or putting out the offering of a bowl of milk for the goddess, painting her eyes on the bows of a boat, or leaving fish behind for her to eat when the fishermen went home. There was plenty of ritual, but little visible evidence for its existence. Archaeology by itself could never have even hinted that, deep down in the minds of the people, the old gods were not forgotten. Great numbers of beautiful churches were raised to the glory of God as Christianity saw it and yet here and there as time went on faces began to peer from corbel or roof boss which were not Christian at all. As dogma increased and became more rigid, so did evidence of hostility to it become more plain. This is bound to happen in any virile race, in which the individual resents being dragooned into uniformity, and no one is more set on uniformity

than the religious bigot, who has convinced himself that God ha
told him in confidence what pleases Him. So, as the Church o
Rome became more apparently omnipotent, in the same degre
more and more men decided that it was a nuisance and a bore. A
translations of Holy Writ appeared in print, after centuries o
concealment in a language which ordinary men did not under
stand, more and more people began to think that Holy Churc
did not always have the right explanation of what God wante
at all. They had been hoodwinked by a caste of professional go
betweens. Trouble was bound to come and long years of bruta
civil wars and wars between nations resulted from it.

The Council of Trent in A.D. 1545–63 had inveighed agains
many of the symbols of re-emerging paganism which th
churchmen thought they could observe, and some of these are th
very things which have caught the eye of students of churc
architecture. The Council, for instance, denounced the represer
tation of the Trinity as a single head formed with two eyes to d
duty for six, three noses and three mouths (Fig. 14 (2)). No
this was the exact manner in which the great Gaulish Trinit
Taranis, Teutates and Esus, had been represented fourteen hur
dred years before (Fig. 14 (1) and (3)). When the Protestan
began to fight for their beliefs, the Rhineland potteries of tl
mid-sixteenth century began to place elaborately moulded ve
sions of this face on their stoneware mugs. They also produc
innumerable jugs and bottles on which a single face appeare
fierce and arrogant. These are the jugs usually spok
of as 'Bellarmines'; but the bearded face is not that of tl
scholarly cardinal, neither is it that of the Duke of Alva as son
supposed. Another set of mugs gives the clue. They are decorat
with scrolls of oak leaves and acorns. In fact the oak tree,
something to do with it, is still found on the German beer mu
of today. But why should the oak appear on a mug for drinki
beer? Surely hops would be more appropriate? The answer
found far back in time. The trinity face is not that of the Chr
tian Trinity; it is the face of Teutates, Taranis and Esus. T
single head is Esus. He, like Zeus, who probably is no mo
than a variant of the name, was the god in the oak tree. He is t
same rustic deity who appeared on the pots of the Roman
Britons and who gazes through the oak leaves in the roof o
village church. The Councillors of Trent were right. There w

aganism in their churches. Once rebellion raised its head, stub-
orn individualists in England, Germany and the Low Countries
rank once more to the great lord of nature, in mugs which
ere protected by his face from any papist slipping some arsenic

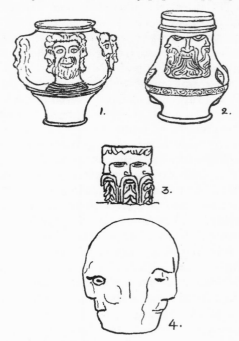

Fig. 14. Return of the old gods.
  (1) Triple head of Taranis, Teutates and Esus on a
      Roman pot from Gaul, c. first century A.D.
  (2) Triple head on Rhenish stoneware pot of mid-six-
      teenth century A.D.
  (3) Triple head carved on a Romano-Gaulish altar
      from Soissons (after O. Brogan).
  (4) Triple head carved in stone from Corleck, Cavan,
      Ireland (after T. E. G. Powell). Presumably Celtic
      pre-Christian Iron Age.

nto the good ale. Thousands upon thousands of these stoneware
ugs, mugs and bottles were shipped into England and they are
nost common in London and the Protestant east. Elizabeth I
ven had them specially made for her household with her cypher

upon them. It would be interesting to know whether she ⟨was⟩
aware whose face was on them. It was the kind of joke which ⟨she⟩
would have appreciated. Most men probably took the face to ⟨be⟩
that of one of their enemies; but many must have known be⟨tter⟩
and, like the Jacobites who succeeded them, drank to the k⟨ing⟩
over the water, not, one suspects, without plenty of gin in it.

Now this Esus must surely be Diana's nature god lover. ⟨In⟩
several places in England, including Glastonbury, great pair⟨s of⟩
oak trees were known as Gog and Magog. Esus is Gog. Ma⟨gog⟩
does not come so well out of the darkness of the Middle A⟨ges.⟩
Long centuries of rule by men had lowered her to second pl⟨ace.⟩
The lover was remembered, while the Queen of Heaven was ⟨to a⟩
great extent forgotten.

The Queen of the May, however, remained at least as long ⟨as⟩
the Jack in the Green. It is the phase of the moon which ⟨is⟩
observed when vegetables are planted and when peats are cut⟨;⟩
then is Macha who sees to this. It is the new moon's face wh⟨ich⟩
you must not see reversed in a glass and the moon's horses⟨hoe⟩
that is hung up for luck. Above all you must not see the n⟨ew⟩
moon through a tree, especially the first new moon of the y⟨ear.⟩
For she is Black Annis and, if you saw here there, she wo⟨uld⟩
drop on you and strangle you. You must not let her shine ⟨on⟩
you while you sleep, or you would become mad, because ⟨you⟩
cannot then rise and do obeisance. Nine times you must bow ⟨to⟩
the new moon; once for each of Brigid's maidens. Then ⟨you⟩
turn your money in your pocket to magic Diana into doubling ⟨it.⟩

After all the years that have passed, the moon still has m⟨any⟩
more superstitious customs relating to her than to the s⟨un.⟩
Lucifer and Beelzebub have not conquered her.

Chapter Eight

THE Celtic Artemis, so we are told, was ruler of all wild animals. Before he could kill any of them, the hunter had to make her an offering. Even a hare, to Roman surprise, had to be indemnified in this way. From what we know and what Roman writers do not seem to have known, the hare, as an attribute of the moon, must have needed a particularly expensive redemption. Be this as it may, the Celtic Artemis was ruler of them all and the classical Diana was Lady of any beast which had part of its anatomy shaped like a sickle moon. Anything with two horns was hers, boars, with their pair of curving tushes, hers, and the horse, with its moon-shaped hooves, particularly hers. But others were hers also, cats for instance and some of the birds. We may say that there was little difference in this respect between the two versions of the Great Mother. Isis joined in with the fishes of the sea.

One of the things one is compelled to notice when looking at the names of the Celtic tribes, whether the ancient ones of Gaul and Britain, or the more modern clans of Scotland, is that some of them are called after animals and others after the various names of the Great Goddess. There are for instance the Chatti, the cats of the Rhineland, and the Boii, the oxen, of Caesar's day; the Cattubellauni, the Cats of War, the Iceni and Epidii, the horse people; the Vacomagi, perhaps Macha's cows or the peoples of the cow plain; the Damnonii, the people of the stag, and the men of the Orcades, the pig islands of the time of Tacitus and Ptolemy. The Brigantes are the people of Brigid and the Tuatha dé Danann those of Danu; while the Caledonii belonged to the Cailleach. There are probably others, but these are the most obvious. All these tribes were presumably named after the

105

Celtic Artemis herself, or her attributes. They must belong to the days before Father gods became most important.

Today there is still clan Chattan, the cat clan, to which the MacPhersons, MacKintoshes, MacGillivrays, MacQueens, Mac-Beans, Keiths, Shaws, Farquharsons and Davidsons belong. Of these clans, portions of what was evidently a great tribe in older days, the arms borne by the chiefs of MacPherson, MacKintosh, MacGillivray and MacBean are a cat of some kind; Shaw and Farquharson have a lion, which is much the same thing, Keith and Davidson a stag's head and MacQueen the head of a wolf. Four then, or six if you can count the lions, still show openly, for the world to see, that they are Cattubellauni, cats of war. While of the other three, who we may perhaps assume to have been detached portions of different tribes, two show the stag of the Damnonii and one the wolf's head of some unknown tribe.

If this is any sort of guide, and correspondence with the Unicorn Herald tells me that he has similar ideas, then clans descended from the ancient Damnonii should include some Gordons, MacKenzies, Frasers, Keiths, Colquhouns and David-sons, although many of these are spoken of with some contempt today as being of Anglo-Norman or Norse origin. The Suther-lands with a cat should once have belonged to Clan Chattan. The boar's head, of what we may think were once the men of Orkney the people of the boar, is that of MacIver, most Campbells, Mac-Kinnons, MacAlpines and some Gordons. It is not strange to find the boar's head on the arms of Malcolmson. They are a sept of the MacLeods of Raasay, who came from Lewis in late medieval times. The sea connection with Orkney is easy. Most unexpected however, is the black bull's head of the MacLeods of Harris, for this is the only clan to still carry what we may assume to have been the ancient sign of the Vaccomagi, who were in eastern Scotland in the days of Ptolemy. There are not many other clans whose arms suggest that they were once people of the Great Mother, the Cailleach of the Caledonii.

The whole idea may be incorrect, but it does suggest a line open to investigation. It hints at tribal movements quite un-thought of today and of the breaking up and reshuffling of ancient units. There is now no chief of the MacEacherns. The tribe has apparently been overrun and absorbed by MacDonalds of Irish origin, as one would have expected from the history of Argyll but of the ancient animal peoples, the Boars, the Stags, the Cats and the Bulls still remain and flourish today. If we knew of a Wolf tribe in the ancient past we could name its descendants. The Cats are not a tribe mentioned in Scotland by Ptolemy; but he has branches of them in Essex and near the Rhine. Caithness is named after them. Possibly they were in process of moving up to the far north, after the defeat of Boadicea's warriors, when Ptolemy's geographical information was collected. Several ancient families in Ireland also bear boars, horses, stags and bulls on their arms. The O'Malley has both horse and boar.

This business of the goddess's beasts can be approached from several angles. First, I think, it is safe to assume that tribes bearing names which relate them to the Great Mother were settled in Britain before the Belgic immigration. They were matriarchal tribes, even if some of them were in process of changing over to the other system when the Romans came. The bulk, if not the whole, of the Pictish nation would have consisted of the matriarchal tribes. If we are to look for traces of their veneration of the Great Mother, then the place to look for them is near the centre of Pictish rule. As it happens there seem to have been two or more such centres. Scone, not far from Perth, was one, and the Inverness district was another at the time of St. Columba. These districts are famed for an unexplained class of antiquities, the Pictish Stones, which I dealt with to some extent in *Gogmagog*. These stones are mostly flat slabs or standing stone pillars and are probably funerary monuments. The most striking thing about them are symbols which seem to be moon and sun emblems and pictures of animals. The more elaborate ones, however, are grouped round a cross. It seems reasonable to suppose that those with animals and symbols alone are purely pagan, while those combining the cross are evidence of dualistic beliefs. Examples exist in which the cross has been added later to an earlier carving. The most frequent animals to be found, on what we may think to be pagan carvings, are stags, horses, bulls, boars, dogs and serpents. The eagle is not infrequent. I have not noticed a cat. The bulls appear to be most common in Aberdeenshire, but the others do not seem to have a local range.

All these beasts belonged to the Cailleach of course. Presumably all animals did, but there are ones which are known to have that association. Now if we return to our clans again we find one, Morrison (Mhic Gille-Morie), which has the serpent as its crest. These Morrisons of Lewis speak of themselves as being descended from a shipwrecked Norseman and are regarded as a Viking clan; but the celebrated Captain Thomas, R.N., who preserved much information about the West Coast, held a different view. In his view the Morrisons, Sons of the Sea, together with the Morgans of Wales and MacNamaras of Ireland, were all septs, or branches, of an old Siol Morganaich and were Lochlannach. The Lochlannach are usually spoken of as Vikings, but the name was in use long before the Vikings came on the scene. Lugh, Nuada and the rest of the Dé Danann gods all came from Lochlinn. There is no reason therefore for assuming a Viking origin for this clan; it is just as likely to have been Pictish. But where was Lochlinn? If it was Norway as is generally assumed, then we should expect to find traces of the old religion there. In the old Norse literature, traces are very scanty, but in the far older rock pictures of Norway and Sweden there is much evidence which might be interpreted in this way. It is, however, so old that, if this is a true link, it goes back in time to our supposed proto-Celtic wave. Then the famous treasures, the sword of Nuada, the never empty cauldron of Dagda and even the Coronation Stone, the Lia Fail itself, came to the British Isles some 1,500 years before the birth of Christ. I find this too difficult to swallow. Dagda and Macha may well be of this age but Lugh, Nuada and the more sophisticated gods must surely belong to the Iron Age, when the sling came into use in war in this country. The evidence of the excavated hill forts, in which the defences were considerably widened to suit the use of this weapon, appears to be quite definite. These gods did not arrive till late in the Iron Age, perhaps 200 B.C. Nuada put out the older sun god, Balor's, eye with a sling-shot.

The difficulty is that so many waves of settlers came into these islands and each time this happened they married some of the women of the older races. These women passed some of their beliefs on to their children and the children learnt other beliefs from the new tribe into which they were born. No religion was ever static, except in areas where no new blood was ever introduced. The priests may have kept what they believed was the pure version of their faith. The congregation never did.

We can separate out various waves of immigration by archaeological study; but though these may give a clear-cut picture of successions of types of pots and tools, they give no true picture of the character of the people. A Brown Bess musket, a Lee Metford rifle and a Bren machine-gun were all used by different generations of Englishmen; but they were also used by different generations of Negroes. Furthermore it is only the doings of the leading families in any tribe which become preserved in history; the origin of their tribesmen may be much the same as their own, or it can be entirely different. It is the name of the leaders by which the tribe was known at a particular time. With a change of leaders the tribal name may become completely altered. Therefore the arms of clan chieftains may be quite as good a guide to the origins of that clan as the recorded genealogies of the chieftains themselves. People speak of Frasers and Gordons as being of Anglo-Norman origin. This may be true of their chiefs and still not true of the clansmen. The stag's head on the crest suggests that these were once a branch of the Damnonii, while the boar's head borne by some Gordons suggests an origin, or at least a period of residence, in the Orkneys. Furthermore suggestions have been made that both clans originated as the Gaulish tribes of Gorduni and Frisii, the Gordon ivy-leaf badge being quoted as the badge of the Gorduni. I do not know where this story of the Gorduni having such a badge is to be found, but I see nothing improbable in the Frasers being once Frisii. Not only were Frisians great sailors on the North Sea, but there is a suggestion in late Roman times that the Firth of Forth was sometimes known as the Frisian Gulf, or Sea. It is by no means improbable that from very early times Frisians had been settling on the east coast of Scotland. The old name of the Frasers was Frizell and their Gaelic name Frisealaich. Many today are called Simpson, after Simon Fraser their former chief.

I think that quite a lot might be learnt by students of heraldry, if they took this matter up on a continental scale. Articles are starting to appear which show that the possibilities are beginning to appeal to more people than the Unicorn Herald. Not only animals on early coats, but suns and moons may suggest associations with the old religious beliefs. No less than three septs originating in heraldic times from the Outer Islands have charges which carry this suggestion: the MacLeods of Harris with their bull, the MacLeods of Raasay with sun in splendour and the Malcolmsons with a boar. It looks as if the mixture of pagan Vikings with the Celts of the islands were more ready than most to take former religious emblems on their arms. In any case the arms of the north are in this respect more interesting than those of England. Why, for instance, has Morison of Bognie in Aberdeenshire a three-faced Saracen's head on his shield? This looks remarkably like the triple-faced head which represents Taranis, Teutates and Esus in pagan Gaul.

This is much too big a subject for me to tackle and only one facet of the study of the Mother Goddess's beasts. These beasts are our real quest at the moment, for they are the guise in which 'the Devil' appeared to his devotees, as is shown clearly in the witch trials. He appeared as a horse, a black dog and so on. There is no mention of this in the accounts of the modern witch rites and we have no idea whether it still happens anywhere in the country. It is, however, worth remarking that it was specially prevalent in the east of Scotland, where the Pictish stones with beasts on them are most numerous today. There must be a connection between the two. The most obvious one surely is that the Devil was representing one of the Great Mother's animals; just as the Maiden of the coven today represents the goddess herself. The Queen of the May in the bad old days, if they were any worse than the present, clearly did the same. The Queen was the most important character, the 'devil' a necessary but less important personage. It was one stage higher up the hierarchy than the single witch and her familiar. At the top of the ladder was Diana herself and her lover, Pan. Perhaps there were other covens in which the 'devil' did not represent the Pan lover at all, but was a Lucifer or Beelzebub. Or perhaps there were yet others in which he stood in place of the Lord of the Underworld. This appears to be the set-up in some modern covens; but there is no means of telling whether the same conditions prevail in all of them. It would be interesting to know.

The pottery of the pagan Saxons in England, as I tried to show in *Gogmagog*, exhibits the same tendency to employ animal forms as is seen on the rather later Pictish stones, while stamps representing the sun and moon are very common. I need not go into this again here. It seems to show, however, that on lowly things like domestic pots, all over the west people liked to place protective charms and these took the form of symbols relating to the old gods. It is not confined to any one age; there are drawings of stags and lunar symbols stamped on the pottery of Iron Age tribes in the Outer Hebrides in the days of Roman rule in Britain, and there are horses of an earlier date drawn on the Celtic pots of Gaul. The whole thing is continuous over many centuries. In Christian Ireland, gods and goddesses appear on metal vessels. Even in medieval England such things seem to occur. Only recently when cleaning some whitewash off a stone, which apparently came from the splay of a fourteenth-century window of a domestic chapel here at Hole, I found a stag scratched with care on the smooth surface. It showed no sign of weathering and the draughtsman may well have known that it would be concealed at once. Some strange things are being learnt from the study of such graffiti in churches, but I will leave them to Mrs. V. Pritchard, who has made them her special study and, I believe, is bringing them out in book form. I do not think, however, I should be speaking out of turn in saying that some graffiti seem to show priests dressing up in animal masks.

To return, however, to this stag from Hole. This is not the work of some naughty child, or unskilled draughtsman. The curves are cut with skill and precision and the drawing is the work of somebody who had had a lot of practice. You cannot walk up to a slab of stone on a wall, pull a knife out of your pocket and produce something of this kind by the light of nature. This is a minor work of art and was put there for a purpose. What that purpose was we can only guess. It is clearly not a part of some vanished scheme of decoration. The stone on which it is drawn is 17 inches long and 11 inches wide and nothing else is cut on it, although on another fragment of the stone there is a dog. I cannot help thinking that, like the tiles with dogs and hares, suns and moons, it had a deeper significance and was one of the goddess's beasts. It is, of course, stretching a point much further than the evidence will allow, but Devon is a land of the Dumnonii. The various versions of Ptolemy sometimes give Damnonii and sometimes Dumnonii and the Scottish branch is presumably an offshoot driven north by the Belgic invasion. If the Scottish branch were, as I think, the people of the Stag, then the Devon one was probably the same, for 'Dumnos' the 'world' seems to make little sense. Is it altogether too wild a guess to suggest that this stag from Hole is the same stag which occurs from time to time on Iron Age pottery in the Hebrides? I have often seen wilder guesses than this in serious works on archaeology. Actual figures of stags turn up in curious places in Britain and are not rare in Roman Gaul. A small bronze casting, looking like a votive object, turned up in the early Christian settlement of Gateholm in Pembrokeshire. In this settlement Major H. E. David and I found evidence for phallic worship in the main building. A fine silver stag was found in the Sutton Hoo ship-burial on what I take to be an iron spear rack, but which is thought by others to have been a standard for use in battle. This is figured in the British Museum's Guide to Sutton Hoo.

One of the favourite beasts of the Mother Goddess in Britain was the boar, or shall we say pig, for both sow and boar figure in old stories. It was the Cailleach's boar which caused the death of Diarmid, the young sun god; pointing I think to a supposed victory of the old matriarchal gods of Scotland over the younger patriarchal gods from Ireland. In Ireland we see the reverse of this picture, when Nuada, one of the newer gods, puts out the eye of Balor, a god of an older hierarchy. It was a sow who used to chase young people down the hills of Wales and gave rise to the saying, 'The Devil take the hindmost'. Boars are not rare in Iron Age art. Bronze statuettes are found and one was drawn on the celebrated Witham shield. They are found as considerable stone carvings in the Celtic art of Gaul, a good one being shown in T. Powell's *The Celts*. I believe that one of these pigs, made of black 'foreign' stone, was found on the island of Barra not so long ago. Its discovery, and the attempt to take a piece broken off it to Glasgow for examination, is said to have raised such terrible gales that it was hastily reburied where it had been found. Figures of pigs are relatively common in pagan Anglo-Saxon ornament and I figured some of them in *Gogmagog*. Perhaps the most remarkable of all, however, was found on the remains of a helmet at Benty Grange, Northumberland, for here was a boar on the crest of the helmet and a small silver Christian cross, not an equal-armed sun symbol, on the front of it. We need to note these pieces of evidence for dualism when we meet them, for they point to two religious charms being considered necessary for a single person. The two beliefs existed side by side, as in the case of King Redwald of East Anglia, who had a Christian altar at one end of his church and one to pagan deities at the other. The Benty Grange helmet may be of seventh-century date.

We can see the boar then being figured as an attribute of the Great Mother from perhaps 200 B.C. right through to the boars on the Pictish stones and to the heraldic devices of Highland chiefs today. Whether it is extinct in English folk-lore, I do not know. But I have never heard tales of it myself.

I do not know for certain whether the cat was a domestic animal in Roman Britain; although I seem to remember having seen cats' footprints on a Romano-British roof tile in some museum. The earliest written mention appears to be in a Welsh law.[1] In this law anyone who killed a royal cat was compelled to pay a fine of so much corn as would cover a cat completely when it was held up by the tail with its nose touching the floor. This does not sound much of a fine, but, judging by the way grain runs out of a hopper, I should think it worked out at about a ton.

The cats, however, of the Cattubellauni and Clan Chattan were, of course, wild cats, a very different proposition from the smug beast curled up in front of my fire. 'Touch not the cat bot a glove,' runs the famous motto of MacPherson, MacKintosh and MacBean; I should hate to touch the only wild cat I have seen in its natural state, even with the thickest hedging glove. I have always been told that they were utterly impossible to domesticate; although somebody has probably succeeded in this unnecessary pursuit by now. Of all the Cailleach's forest creatures, the wild cat gives the best representation of her murderous ferocity.

I do not know any early pictures of wild cats and by the time they do appear in Irish art, well on in Christian days, they were probably domestic beasts. 'I and Padur ban, my cat,' wrote the old Irish scribe, ''tis a like task we are at.'

The ram may be most important as a pointer towards the area in which the developed Mother Goddess religion originated. I am thinking of Colchis and the Golden Fleece. The ram is common in Celtic art in Gaul and its head is often used on the ends of bracelets and suchlike ornaments. I have even found a specimen in what I took to be the grave of a Cattubellaunian

[1] Laws of Howell Dda, prince of Gwynneth.

113

chieftain in England. The ram, however, is more closely associated with the male god than with the Great Mother; although I do not think that this is a very great matter, for with the change-over to the greater importance of the father, many of the mother's attributes became linked with him. We find the ram then associated with variants of the sun god; everybody must have heard of Jupiter Ammon in Egypt. Like the goat, another of the Cailleach's beasts, which is just another sheep, he is looked upon now as somewhat indecent and deeply linked with the popular idea of devils and witches. In olden times, however, he had not fallen to this lowly estate and to this day remains as the symbol of Mars. There were no ram or goat clans in the British Isles, or if there were such tribes, no mention has survived. For some reason, however, which is not understood, the ram's head became attached to the body of the serpent. Not only is the serpent found quite often on the Pictish stones, but it is also one of the Cailleach's beasts and is frequent on Anglo-Saxon pottery, as I have mentioned already. The serpent is the crest of the Morrisons of Lewis.

Although the adder is venomous, its bite is seldom fatal to man and it is not very often seen. It is, however, a sinister beast and well suited to the Cailleach when she was a destroyer. Kali, her Indian counterpart, has a girdle of snakes. The adder always appears when you least expect it. You nearly put your hand on it on a bank, or sit on a wall and see it peering at you with darting tongue. My wife has a great dislike of them. Once when crossing a dry bog in Mull, near to where the sinister black shape of the Cailleach's Head juts into the Western Ocean towards Coll, she remarked, 'I don't like this place. I am sure there are adders here.' I replied that I had tramped innumerable miles in Mull without once seeing the infamous Mull adder. As I said this, I looked down to see one curled up on a tussock of grass at my feet. That is the way of it. But there are no adders in the Outer Islands. The Morrisons got their serpent elsewhere.

On the celebrated Gunderstrup bowl in Copenhagen, a great silver cauldron probably made by Celts in Central Europe and frequently figured, Cernunnos is shown with antlered head and lunar torque, holding a ram-headed serpent in his hand. I showed a drawing of this in *Gogmagog*. It seems probable that this is another example of the struggle for supremacy between

114

patriarchy and matriarchy and compares with the story of Diarmaid and the Cailleach's boar. In this case Cernunnos has the Cailleach's serpent by the throat and her lunar symbol in his hand. He is represented as taking over her functions and her animals as well. When the ram-headed serpent appears in later Gaulish art, it is associated with male deities, but in Scotland it remained the property of the Cailleach. The change in the sex of the gods reached Gaul before Britain. But though the representations of the gods in Gaul in the Roman period show that this had taken place to a very wide extent, yet after Roman rule collapsed it was Diana who survived longer than any other. I use the name Diana in its widest sense, for the Breton blessing of the fleets of terraneuvas which set out to fish on the Grand Banks of Newfoundland today, is almost detail for detail the blessing of the Mediterranean fleets at the beginning of the sailing season, as is described by Apuleius in *The Golden Ass*. This was in honour of Isis. We will, however, deal with the Isis question later on.

Horses were of great importance to the Celtic world; on account of their moon-shaped hooves they were Diana's. It was with war chariots and wagons that they fought their way across Europe. Long before the Transvaal Boers, the Celts made use of the wagon laager to defend their moving camp. It was with chariots that the Aryans appeared on the plains of India. Somewhere on the Steppes of Asia, the chariot of war must have been evolved from a primitive cart with solid wheels. Who made this revolutionary discovery of a rapidly moving platform for use in war is not known, but this, together with the invention of the sea-going ship, changed the face of the world. Its weakness was that it was too wide and the horses were too far in front of the driver for a real cavalry charge to be made against well-trained infantry armed with missile weapons. It was useless against Roman legionaries; although, as Caesar tells us, when they first met it in Britain they were alarmed by the whirring wheels and the gymnastics of the warriors running out along the poles and slashing with their great swords. The chariot was slowly pushed north by newer methods of warfare and the use of cavalry, until we hear the last of it used against Agricola in Angus. In Ireland it survived for much longer and the bards told remarkable tales of heroes jumping their chariot teams over fallen logs and similar evolutions. These tales, faithfully written down by Christian monks about their ancestors, can still be read by us today. Chariots, as a means of rapid transport, remained in use in the Middle Ages and were presumably the ancestors of the gigs and dog-carts in which we drove as children.

In Gaul, the horse goddess, Epona, which is simply Gaulish for mare and not her secret name, was venerated by Roman cavalry regiments and accepted in Rome itself. As I have said before, Epona's mother was a mare and her father a male human figure (Fig. 2 (a)). This survival of totemistic marriage has already been discussed. All these animal companions of god and goddess were once totems.

At this point it struck me that it would be interesting to have a look at the arms of the Duke of Norfolk, the creation of whose dukedom dates from 1483. It was no surprise, after what has already come out of the heraldic side of the story, to find that one of his crests was a silver horse with a sprig of oak in its mouth. It is pleasing, even if it should be but a coincidence, that the chief peer in the land of the Iceni, the horse people, should combine on one of his helms the horse of the Great Mother and the oak of Esus, or Pan. I do not think that these things can be coincidences, there are too many of them. They are clues to scraps of ancient history, waiting for us to pick them out. All through their remarkable history the Howards have been noted for their adherence to old causes. Is it surprising that their arms should indicate a similar tendency nearly five hundred years ago? The Howards were Yorkist and it was to the gold angel of the Yorkist king, Edward IV, that the sun symbol was added beside the head of Michael, or Lugh. The symbol was not on the earlier angel of the Lancastrian king, Henry VI, although the rest of the design was much the same. 'Jackie of Norfolk be not too bold,' read the alarming doggerel flung into the Duke of Norfolk's tent before the battle of Bosworth Field, 'for Diccon thy master is bought and sold.' Yet Jackie ignored it and died with his master on the field. This was a fine piece of loyalty and his son, who was taken prisoner at Bosworth, well deserved the victory he won at Flodden twenty-eight years later. It is all in keeping with Kipling's view of the grammerie of Merlin's Island: 'Old wars, old peace, old arts that cease and thus was England made.' It is all silly sentimentality I suppose, but why must we forget loyalty and heroism even if it was a long time ago. Should the study of antiquity be robbed of these, it would not be worth anything at all. If there had been no Flodden, 'The Flowers of the Forest', one of the most beautiful laments, would never have been written.

If you look at history as if it were a huge piece of woven material, you can pick out strands running through the pattern in both directions. If you had all these strands in your hand, some made of metal instead of wool, you could reconstitute the pattern from a fragment by the bends in the metal ones. This has been done with gold strips fallen from a vanished brocade. If we can get enough strips and not just follow a single one, we will be able to do the same. History, archaeology, folk-lore, heraldry, anthropology and many more threads are in our hands, but the threads are broken in many places. If we spread out, study, and juggle these threads, patches of pattern begin to form. It is up to anyone to say we have got it wrong, but not to question the possibility of success. Without the many strands, there is not the slightest hope of getting more than a single pretty piece of metal with an irregular series of ups and downs on it. The difficulty today is to find enough people to take a number of strips in their hands and try to make out a pattern from them. Far too many are tied to a single strip and measuring with the greatest accuracy its ups and downs and the exact composition of the metal. For this reason I pick up every strip I can lay hands on, including an unorthodox but most useful one called Inherent Probability. Some may not belong to the same piece of cloth and will never fit at all. Others will be broken in vital places. But when you find several which do fit so that a recognizable pattern begins to emerge, then you can be pretty sure that the pattern is right, for it would not fit together in any other way. Our heraldic strand fits into the inequalities of the historical, archaeological, anthropological and folk-lore strands. This can hardly be coincidence. But let others try it. Then we would begin to learn something.

As usual I have been diverted from my train of thought. Let us get back to our horses.

The Celts for many centuries rubbed shoulders with the Scythians of the lands northward of the Black Sea. The Scandinavian gods of Aasgard came from there and who today can be

117

certain, without hearing him speak, that a fair-haired, long-chinned Norseman is not a fair-haired, long-chinned Celt? The Celts borrowed their trews from the Scythians, for the garb of old Gaul did not include the kilt. They may well have borrowed the horse and perhaps their religion also.

The Scythians had methods of sacrificing horses which were remarkably unpleasing. They threaded the unfortunate beasts on long poles and raised them into the air. Readers who wish to learn about the extreme antiquity of this practice and also of its survival down to the days of photography in inner Asia, should consult the late Sir Ellis Minns's *Scythians and Greeks*. The reason I mention this is because the Irish Great Mother, Badb, had a magic horse, which was threaded on a chariot pole, fastened by a peg on its forehead. This must surely have been a ghost horse, sent to her by sacrifice in the Scythian manner. According to Herodotus, many men and horses were sacrificed at the funeral of a Scythian king, stuffed and pegged up round his burial mound. The whole group was probably intended to accompany him as a present to their deity. It is a revolting picture, but many abominable deeds have been performed in the name of some misguided interpretation of the wishes of gods. Horse sacrifice, presumably learnt from the same source as that of the Scythians, went with the Aryan warriors into India. We have already discussed the hippogamous ritual which attended it at the Asvamheda ceremony. These two rites, hippogamy and sacrifice of horses, then seem to have been spread in two directions from a common source of origin. Horse sacrifice may never have been actually performed on a pole in Ireland; but a myth remained. Both rites are, to say the least of it, so peculiar that they cannot be the result of independent invention. Two rings of thought, presumably with a common point of origin, have spread outwards till they are now thousands of miles apart; for the last pole sacrifices of horses were performed in the Altai region. These are no doubt very early waves, going back in time to that of the early use of war chariots. We may safely say that their origin was not later than the early Bronze Age, perhaps 4,500 years ago, and that the Great Mother's association with the horse is older than that. I think this is a very modest estimate. We can believe probably that the association of horse and Great Mother is as old as the Aurignacian hunters of the Palaeolithic caves of France, who lived on the horse. If this is so, then the origins of Diana and Pan are contemporary. In fact the origin of this side of the witch religion is so old that years do not matter at all.

With the exception of those connected with the Moon Herself, there are probably more traces of veneration paid to the horse surviving in Britain today than to any other object. There are so many superstitions that, although I brought a number of them together in *Gogmagog*, I shall not attempt to enlarge on them here. Everyone must know about wishing when you see a white horse and doing so before you think of its tail. They must have heard of the 'Horseman's oath' and know superstitions about picking up horseshoes. They know about Lady Godiva and the lady riding to Banbury Cross and they have seen the great white horse at Uffington, whose very name is more likely to have originated in a corruption of 'epos' than in that of the name of some imaginary Saxon farmer. They may not have heard, however, of the Mari Llwyd, the grim horse's skull on a pole, which is rushed through Welsh houses at Christmastide and seems to carry a faint reflection of the horror of the pole sacrifice.

Weird ceremonial horses, usually known as hobby horses, still appear in various parts of Britain, from Kent to Cornwall and in the north-west. Of these the Padstow horse, which processes in the streets on May 1st, is perhaps the most remarkable, for its head is by no means unlike Magog's beast on the hill outside Wandlebury Camp. This, however, is a horse connected with the sea, for the performance is carried out by fishermen. It is not surprising, for the Cailleach was intimately connected with the sea as well as the land. Her breasts are only found on islands today, and her head projects into the ocean. Her husband was a sea god and she washed her blanket in Corrievreckan. Observers have noted traces of fertility rites in the Padstow ceremony. We should not forget that, in Greek myth, Neptune turned himself into a stallion when he wished to seduce an unwilling maiden and that his white horses still cover the sea in a breeze of wind.

Horse races and processions figured largely in connection with the old pagan festivals of Britain and are recorded from unexpected places, as well as near the great Iron Age hill forts. One of the most curious is the one which used to take place on the island of Canna, on Lugh, or Michael's day. There the men took their wives, sweethearts, or neighbours' wives on their horses and raced round the village, the ceremony ending in a feast provided by the women. The uneven character of the ground where the village once stood makes it very hard to see why horses were employed at all, unless they formed a necessary part of the ceremony. Two ancient crosses of late Pictish type stood in the neighbourhood of the ancient church, which was deliberately destroyed in the nineteenth century. One cross still stands with a man riding a horse, and with other animals on its face. The other, perhaps one of the most unusual roods in Britain, has a huge serpent on one side with the figure of Christ, and interlaced serpents on the other side (Fig. 15). Many small crosses from the neighbourhood, collected by Mrs. Campbell of Canna, testify to the high antiquity of the site which we may believe to have been a pagan sanctuary before the coming of Christianity. Much might have been learnt here, but for the virulent antipathy felt for it by a former owner. Not only did he destroy the church and smash the memorials, but he removed the village and ploughed everything up. But a belief in the sith, the so-called fairies, still clings to the place.

Of course we are very near the end of an age, and all this kind of thing will soon be gone. That is why it is so important to snatch up our strands of information while there is still time to do so. More than this, I do not think that future generations will have the right background from which to interpret the strands if they do happen to notice them. The process of bringing in a uniform standard of living tends to produce a dismal uniformity of knowledge, or of ignorance.

The bull is definitely less important than the horse. Bulls are quite common in Celtic art on the Continent and in Britain itself. Wars were fought in ancient Ireland for the possession of bulls of outstanding quality. The Druids used white oxen when collecting the mistletoe. Fine bulls are found drawn on the Pictish stones. The bull is a strong and virile beast and of massive size, and yet he is uncommon in folk-tale or superstition. There is a Golden Calf buried near Goodwood racecourse and there are water bulls in Scotland. Leaning on the rail of my boat in Loch na Beiste in Skye, I once asked old John Robertson, whose birthplace was just a few miles over the hill, what was the beast after which the loch was named. 'I mind, boss,' he said, 'that an old

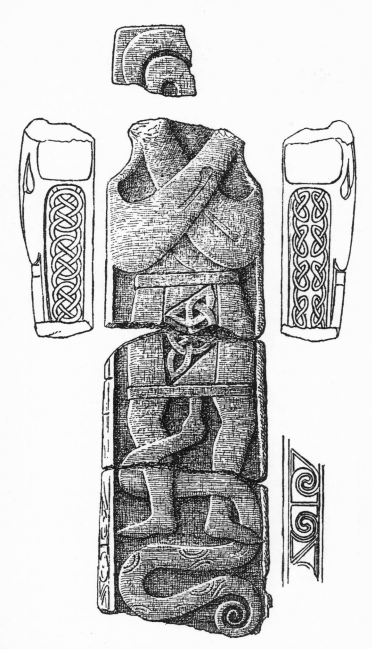

Fig. 15. Stone cross-shaft from Isle of Canna. Length 3 ft. 4½ in.
Fragment of head of the cross apparently shows a second serpent.
Date uncertain, perhaps ninth century A.D.

woman told me when I was a lad [he was about eighty at the time] that it was a bull with one leg.' That is as near as I have ever got to any stories about bulls. There are no bulls in pagan Saxon ornamental art and I cannot think of any in Irish art. There are, however, quite a number of Romano-British ones and some of these have three horns and are important in their own particular way. The bull figured largely in Mithraic ritual. Occasionally you find the term used to describe a man of outstanding immorality. The name of ram is used in the same connection. As far as I can see no ghost bull and few figures of bulls have survived the Roman period. There may be occasional exceptions, like the armorial bulls of the Nevilles and those of Clan Torquil, the MacLeods of Lewis, whose name may not come from Thorkel, or Thorketil, but from 'torus', a bull; but these are few and far between. We do know, however, that the natives of Dorset, near the Cerne Giant, had a carved bull's-head mask, known as the Oozer, which is figured in Margaret Murray's *The God of the Witches*. We know also from Sir James Fraser that bulls' skins were worn at the Hogmanay ceremony in Scotland. These are enough for us to keep the bull on our list.

I have already talked about ghost dogs and the relationship between dogs and the ancient gods. Dogs are common on the Pictish stones. I have found one stamped on a pagan Saxon pot and they are common in the Christian art of the whole of the British Isles in the Dark Ages. There seems to be no particular reason why a man should draw a dog more frequently than a bull, except that it is more companionable. But there is no need to say more than this. We have stories of supernatural dogs all over the country. The Devil sometimes took the form of a dog at witches' sabbats. The dog was Diana's messenger. There is no doubt at all that the beast figured at all periods since the worship of the Great Mother arrived in Britain. We can leave it at that without turning to nursery rhymes, heraldry or any other aid. The beast figured frequently as a witch's familiar and the name of one, 'Elva', the sister-in-law of Lugh, has actually been preserved to form a link between the old gods and the witch cult in this country as well as in Italy.

As far as I am aware only three animals exist in popular belief as ghosts. These are the dog, the white horse and the hare. Of these three, the hare was the form most frequently adopted by a witch if she did not wish to be recognized. Like the horse and dog it was a beast closely associated with Diana. The psychologist, Layard, wrote a book on the subject, which I had at one time, but which, like so many of my books, appears to have been borrowed. However the hare in the classical world appears to have been a symbol of the soul. In the Gaelic world the soul was a butterfly. People in Ireland within the last century have claimed to have seen a butterfly emerging from the mouth of a dying person. I have no reason for supposing that this observation was correct.

The hare is hardly the sort of animal which any warrior would willingly choose to have emblazoned on his shield, or by which a tribe would enjoy being called. One remembers the story of the unfortunate Frenchmen at the time of Edward III's first campaign in France, who were knighted in a hurry because the English put up a hare and their shouts gave the impression of an impending attack. The derisive epithet 'Knights of the Hare' clung to them ever afterwards. So, except for hunting scenes, there are few pictures of hares to give us any clue. It is, however, common enough in folk-lore for this to be of little account. We know that it was a beast of the Great Mother in Gaul, for it is the only animal mentioned by name for which the hunter had to ask Artemis's permission before he killed it. This ties in well enough with the witch familiars.

Excluding all the lions and other foreign beasts over which Diana held sway in warmer lands, I think we have produced enough evidence to show that the same was true of the Great Mother in Celtic countries. Not only that, either in the guise of the Devil, or the witches' familiar, she retained this property right down to modern times. There appears to be no break in the succession, for if there are gaps in one series they are made good in others. If proof were needed that Diana of the Witches is the same as Danu, Macha, the Badb, the Cailleach, Magog and all the rest, the animals seem to provide it.

Chapter Nine

WHEN Tacitus wrote his account of the Northern peoples, he expressed surprise that the Suevi should worship Isis and that her symbol was a light war galley. Although we live nearly two thousand years later, I think we know a little more about it than he did and our knowledge is largely due to archaeological research. The reason why the symbol of Isis among the ancestors of the Swedes should have been a galley is quite easy to see. The high stem and stern of such a vessel suggested the horns of Isis's moon, just as the shape of a horse's hoof suggested it. The wish was father to the thought. Seamen wanted the Great Mother to protect their ships and they saw her sign in their shape. It is as easy as that.

In parts of southern Norway and Sweden there are places where the rocks are covered with engraved drawings of ships, which fully confirm the information given to Tacitus. They appear to range over at least 1,500 years in time and to still have been made in the Iron Age. The heraldic strand picks them up again in the arms of families in Orkney and the west of Scotland. Of course we may say that anyone who lives near the sea and sees people using it all the time, will naturally draw ships, or put them on his coat of arms if he happens to own them. But this does not explain Tacitus's observation that Isis was worshipped in this form. The observations of archaeologists have clearly shown that Tacitus was right in one particular and he was presumably right in the other. The word 'Isis' was only his definition of a moon goddess connected with the sea, a Cailleach in fact. We do not know what name was really used by the ancient Swedes and it probably would be of no help to us if we did. We will call her Isis in this chapter; although I have no doubt she is the same Great Mother whom we have been watching all this time and that she was just as much the goddess of the horse, or bull, or cat, as she was of the war galley.

Seamen, however, are somewhat a race apart and are more international than any other class of men. The worship of Isis, as I have suggested before when I mentioned the blessing of the Breton fleet of Terraneuvas, was hardly different in the eastern Mediterranean of classical times from that of the Christian Bretons of today. Names only have changed, the ritual remains. Even in England, the mayor of Colchester, who goes out and eats his oysters at the opening of the fishing season, is taking the place of the priests of Isis, who figured so vividly in *The Golden Ass*. This is one of the really dramatic survivals of an ancient custom, and it was as widespread. In the north of Lewis, not so very long ago, men waded into the sea, poured beer into it and implored Shony (Sithonaid?), the holy one, to give them of its fruits. This is precisely the same ritual, although curtailed through time, as

Fig. 16.

(1) Bronze figure of Isis type (a crescent moon has probably been broken from the front of her diadem) from the temple of the Seine. Duck's head and tail on the galley which is clearly ancestral to the Northern Longships.

(2) 'Isis' bird and fish on a modern Highland coaster (Ben Hiant).

that described by Apuleius. And yet we are told that the people of Lewis are mostly descendants of Norsemen, while they have the serpents and bulls of the Cailleach, and call on the holy one in Gaelic. The Norse strain, which was undoubtedly

125

there in the ninth century, must have been largely bred out through the centuries. The Lewismen take to the sea and the Skyemen to the army, but so would you if you lived in one or the other of the islands. It is a topographical and not an ethnographical matter.

So there we are with Isis being worshipped in such diverse places as Sweden, Brittany and Lewis, and are faced with Tacitus's problem of how she get there at all (Fig. 16).

The answer seems to be that she got there at a very early period and came, not with the true Iron Age Celts, but with the early Bronze Age proto-Celtic wave of civilization. The clue must be of course in the ships. In *Gogmagog* I made some attempt to identify the origin of the particular form of ship drawn on the Scandinavian rocks and was led towards the coasts of Asia Minor. It was in this comparatively large and mountainous area that the Hatti, or Hittites, seem to have originated, whose gods left their names on the tablets of Bogaz-Keui. Fourteen hundred years before the birth of Christ, Indra, Mitra and Varuna were already names of importance. Baal and Ashtoreth apparently originated in the mountains of Asia Minor, while ships bearing some resemblance to those on the Scandinavian pictures were in use on the southern coast. Celtic legends of their origin preserved in the Barddas say that the Cwmry came from a summer-land of lakes and mountains. The Celtic festivals indicate an origin among pastoral peoples, who distinguished between summer and winter grazing. Scraps of information begin to pile up. There are others. Asia Minor is more or less halfway between India and Britain. Only a people used to mountains and sea coasts would deliberately go to countries like Scandinavia and Scotland. The originators of Cailleach and Isis beliefs must have been both hillmen and seamen. They cannot have been people of inland plains. This rules out areas like the foothills of the Alps, Himalayas, Altai and so on. But it does not exclude Asia Minor, an area in which religions seem often to have been born. But did the peoples of Asia Minor use the sea? We can take it from Greek myth that they did and a sea, too, which can be remarkably formidable at times.

When the Argonauts had made their voyage to Colchis, stolen the Golden Fleece and fled with it and the king's daughter, who was probably even more important, they were pursued on the sea and only saved by human sacrifice of the king's son. How could they have been pursued unless the people of Colchis were seamen and had fast vessels? There are several important clues in this story. The first is the Fleece itself. It is an emblem of the trade of Colchis, for fleeces were used by gold-washers to collect the particles of gold brought down by the streams. Jason was a Greek pirate, no less, and he came to get possession of the gold-washing industry. At that time it was a habit of adventurous Greeks to go to places where matriarchy still prevailed, marry the heiress and so succeed to the throne. Jason did this, but failed to establish himself and fled with the heiress, hoping to return and claim the throne later. But the expedition was a failure and the Greeks never did obtain Colchis. I am writing as if this were a story of an episode in the lives of one set of people. Of course it was nothing of the kind. It is the legend of an attempt made by Greek adventurers to seize an important source of wealth and it was attended by war and failure. Colchis was too rich and powerful to be taken as Troy was. Nobody has paid very much attention to the possibilities of Colchis, but they will have to do so.

Recently some splendid graves have been published from Dorak, near the sea of Marmara. These contained swords, spears and daggers of Early Bronze Age type, but with blades of gold and silver. They are weapons of shapes which would be dated in England to about 1400 B.C. But this is a thousand years too late for those at Dorak. In one grave were found five gold and silver statuettes of a goddess and her attendants; no gods. On one of the silver sword-blades are engraved many ships. In these graves we seem to see representations of both Isis and her ships, for the goddess (Fig. 11 (a)) has a hair-style and ornaments resembling those of the Iron Age figure from Faardal in Denmark (Fig. 11 (b)). The hands indicating the breasts and the hair in a pig-tail down the back suggest a family relationship to Magog at Wandlebury (Fig. 12). Recently James Mellart has found the Dorak hair-style some thousands of years earlier on pottery figurines of the Neolithic period. This indicates that both ships and goddess came to Scandinavia from Asia Minor at a very early period.

Chapter Ten

THE value of all research connected with the study of Antiquity lies in the lessons which can be drawn from the way our ancestors behaved in given circumstances. It is otherwise simply the collection of information of entertainment value and its practitioners no more than public entertainers. Many people with a smattering of psychology regard archaeology and its kindred subjects as no more than an escape from the troubles of the modern world. But there is more to it than that and the lessons it teaches are by no means negligible, especially to townsmen, who are on the whole pretty helpless creatures. Archaeology has shown how through long ages man steadily forced the powers of nature to serve his ends; until he reached a stage where he can destroy the whole lot of them should that fancy take him. Whether it has really produced an evolutionary story of man himself according to the Darwinian pattern is more than doubtful and Darwin's theories are no longer the ultimate truth that they were once thought to be. Many people are beginning to feel that, although there is such a thing as evolution, it needs some external push to make it work. The story of the neck of the giraffe, which grew continually longer by the process of 'natural selection' and 'survival of the fittest', aroused considerable amusement when someone asked what happened to the children before their necks were long enough to reach the top branches of the trees. When scientists, to whom the ultimate truth was to be revealed when they could examine the smallest forms of matter, reached a stage in which they could distinguish no difference between it and mind, the materialism of the last century became obsolete. It will take some time to die, but it is already doomed. We have reached therefore a time in which it is worth while examining ancient beliefs to see whether those that held them had any ideas which might help us today. Things which appeared to be primitive superstition, when science knew all the answers, may not now be as stupid as they seemed fifty years ago.

It is hard to make a study of this kind impartially, for the results are bound to be coloured by the point of view held by the observer at the time he makes it. This is true of every study of the past, for the whole can never be known. All history is a summary of what is known, distorted to some extent by the opinions held by the man who writes it. If he is a socialist, he will write it in quite a different manner from a conservative. Things which appear laudable to one age seem abominable to another. You can say that the battle of Naseby was fought in 1645 and you can walk over the fields and pick up a musket ball to show that it was fought on a particular piece of ground. But no historian agrees with another as to what went on in the heads of the commanding officers and still less as to the thoughts of the rank and file. Yet this was a most important event and only a little more than three hundred years ago. How much less reliable must be our guesses at the reasons for the actions of prehistoric man. Therefore what I have to say in this section is no more than a summary of what I happen to think at this particular time. It is quite possible that further evidence may show me that I am wrong in these views and then I shall change them with no regret. It is the true answer which is being sought and not a pat on the head for writing a passable exam paper.

We will start with what appears to be a fundamental faith of Dianic believers. They hold that men are born again on this earth and that intercession with their goddess will ensure that the Lord of the Underworld, whose job it is, will put them back into it among the friends they loved in this life. This belief is known as reincarnation and differs from what is presumably an elaboration of it, known as transmigration. In transmigration you will not only be born again, but if you have done badly in this life you may find yourself born in animal form. This disturbing belief may picture the cat snoring in front of the fire as your late grandmother, or a worm on the lawn as your uncle. You go up and down the scale according to how you progress in your earthly life. People holding this faith cannot kill anything for fear of it being some friend or relation. Transmigration was

129

accepted as a dogma by the Druids and the Pythagorean school of Greeks. It is also held by many Hindus today. The classical peoples were unable to account for how the belief was found among the peoples of Gaul and Britain. It seems probable that it was brought into Britain by the Iron Age Celts and came from the same central source as that which exported it to both Greece and India.

Reincarnation, a perfectly plausible idea to most people, was held by the Christian Church until about A.D. 500. It was then declared a heresy. At some date, apparently not long after this, an addition to the creed substituted the belief that men rose again with their bodies. This idea, palpably absurd to anyone who has seen the effects of high explosive, has only recently lost ground. Reincarnation is one of the main doctrines of Buddhists. Most of their energies are directed towards freeing themselves from what is called the 'Wheel of Life', that is from an unbearable succession of lives spent in pain and misery.

In recent times the doctrine of reincarnation has received a remarkable impetus from the results of psychical research. A very good summary and discussion of this work is to be found in R. C. Johnson's *The Imprisoned Splendour*. The results have all been obtained and still are being obtained at what may be termed second hand. The workers use what we would call a 'medium', a person who is known in their terminology as a 'sensitive'. The work has been carried out with the greatest competence and scientific care. If it were only a matter of studying atoms, or fleas, it is improbable that anyone would question the findings. The information obtained through the mediums, either by direct speech or through what is known as automatic writing, purports to come from persons who are no longer in this world, but have passed from it to another plane of life. The most notable of these communicators is supposedly the celebrated Cambridge personality, F. W. H. Myres, who died in 1902.

Myres is believed to have transmitted a great bulk of information through the writings of various sensitives. Most elaborate means were devised for checking and cross-checking these writings. Messages with difficult allusions were split up among several automatic writers, collected at a central point, joined together again in one message and then studied with care.

It is hard to see a flaw in the results. But the reader must form his own opinion on this. I am not taking sides. This is a study of primitive religion and not a work on psychical research.

The picture derived from the study of the information purporting to have been supplied by Myres and many others, is most interesting, for it corresponds closely to the beliefs held by many religions and is of very great antiquity. The only possible explanation appears to be that all these religions originated in the same way. That is they were derived from information supplied by mediums. If this is the correct interpretation, it is another very strong argument for regarding the Myres type of communication as correct. If it were not so, we ought surely to find great variations.

The picture of the next stage of existence derived from the automatic communications is briefly summed up as follows:

The whole Universe from galaxy to electron is the product of a Universal Mind and it is only kept in being by the thought of that mind. A whole hierarchy of thinking units in descending grades of intelligence exists throughout the Universe and all can be described as part of the Universal Mind. Each grade of intelligence is a component of a higher grade. Some capacity for thought exists in the smallest particle of matter, which is thus, in a sense, a mind. However dead and inert some objects may appear to us, yet each object contains untold millions of tiny foci of thought. Man on earth appears to be at the lowest stage of permanent, that is immortal, intelligence. He, as an individual, is one unit in a larger mind, which is known as a Group Soul. This in itself is far below the highest grade of intelligence; but will ultimately raise itself to a higher standard. The Group Soul has a varying number from twenty or thirty to one thousand human souls belonging to it. It is born as a thought of the Universal Mind, perfect in itself, but without knowledge. Wisdom and knowledge have to be collected for it by its component souls on lower levels of existence. Its component souls retain their own individuality, but are part of the Group Soul. They are immortal.

There are several planes to be passed through by each individual soul before it gains complete contact with its present Group Soul. When it has done this, the evolutionary process still continues, but is no concern of us here. The reason we cannot make direct contact with our particular Group Soul on this plane

131

of earth is that it exists at a higher frequency than we do. Our bodily senses have only a very narrow range and we are unable to see, feel, or hear innumerable vibrations which are passing through us all the time. Rare individuals, either as a result of lengthy techniques, or some freak of their bodily construction, do make contact with their Group Soul by stepping up the rate of their vibrations. The contact with their Group Soul appears to them to be contact with God. Since the group belonging to the Group Soul consists of both male and female members, both male and female deities are reported from time to time. Real contact with God is on so far higher a plane as to be inconceivable to us. Even then it would only be contact with the entity responsible for running this particular universe. There is no need at this stage for anyone to bother his head about it.

It is told that our earthly plane of existence is the first and that real contact with the Group Soul is not established till the fourth plane. There are, however, stages in the planes and opinions differ as to how many there are. Up to the fourth plane, however, all these worlds, if we may call them so, are located in the same portion of space as the visible earth. They are invisible to us owing to the difference in the rates of vibration.

Man, we are informed, consists of three coexistent bodies, of which only the earthly body is known to us. The soul is wrapped up in these bodies. Terminology is particularly tiresome here and different writers give different names to these bodies. They appear, however, to correspond closely to insect metamorphosis.

A considerable body of information is thought, however, to have been obtained about life on the third plane, which is relevant to our investigation. The third plane is obviously the Heaven of many religions. It is said to be not at all unlike the version of earth on which we live, but is more beautiful and largely devoid of stress and strain. There is little incentive to sharpen one's wits. People create their own homes and surroundings for their own pleasure as they do on earth, but there is no urgency or drive about it and no possibility of being bodily hurt. Since the whole object of existence is, it seems, to advance the intellectual power of the individual and through it, by the pooling of knowledge, of the Group Soul, the third plane is rather a quiet back-water.

People may live on it and enjoy it for long periods, but,

sooner or later, the urge to rise to higher planes drives each individual either to force himself to go up higher, or to return to earth once more to sharpen his intelligence, for further advance, in that more drastic environment. The communications of Myres and others state that this reincarnation does not normally occur more than four times; although occasional cases are found in which persons with special interests on earth may return as many as nine times. It is clear moreover from the communications that the urge to be born again and even the choice of parentage is thought to be in the hands of each individual and is nothing to do with the parents. Their part in the matter is simply to provide a body with which the individual concerned can be born. The individual's choice of a future earthly body is limited however by what is known as the 'Law of Karma'. This is a kind of sum of cause and effect of all thoughts and actions, good or bad, in previous earthly lives. Karma affects the whole of the individual's life on earth. It is said that one individual of a group can take over the karma that another has built up. Thus a 'first-timer' would take over the karma of an individual of the same group who had completed his turns of duty.

Members of a group are to be found on all levels up to and including the one above the Astral (third), for the Group Soul as a whole has to wait until all members of the group have completed their passages through the lower levels. When this is complete the group as a whole can move up to a higher level. Occasional individuals are found who are completely incapable of advancing. These are simply thought about no longer and fall out of existence.

Perhaps the most important piece of information for our study is that very rare individuals are occasionally created at a higher level than the Group Soul. They go down to earth for a single life of great importance and return after it to a high level again. These are the great religious teachers of the world and are known to Hindu religion as 'Avatars'. Christ, Krishna and Gautama Buddha are obvious examples. However, it seems to be that the individual dimly portrayed in the witches' Vangelo Aradia was another.

This is a very brief, but I hope comprehensive and understandable, summary of what virtually amounts to a new faith, produced by the efforts of highly skilled workers on the subject of psychical research. The care taken to ensure that it is correct has been enormous. But with so intangible and important a subject, which may well be incapable of scientific proof, everyone must form his own opinion.

We will now try to compare this summary with those of other beliefs and see what comes of it. Perhaps it is as well to begin with the Druids. Their beliefs, as I explained earlier in this book (p. 29), have only survived in relatively modern works; but internal evidence suggests that they are perfectly genuine survivals. They may well have become somewhat garbled through centuries of repetition, but nevertheless the main ideas are probably correct. The Druidic conception of the world consisted of three concentric globes, the centre of which is Cythraul, the Abyss. Outside the Abyss is the first circle known as Annwn, which corresponds with the plane of earthly existence. Outside this again comes the circle, or sphere, of Gwynvyd, which we may regard as the third plane, or astral, of the psychical research theory. At the extreme outer limit of Gwynvyd comes the sphere of Ceugant, which corresponds to the higher levels of eternity.

God, according to Druidic belief, created all living things from the smallest particles of light and 'in every particle there is a place wholly commensurate with God, for there is not, and cannot be, less than God in every particle of light, and God in every particle; nevertheless God is only one in number'. God created all living things in the circle of Gwynvyd, on the astral plane. But the living things wished to be Gods and attempted to cross the sphere of Ceugant, the planes above the astral, and so they fell down to Annwn, the earth. Here, once again, we find Lucifer, the being created from light, attempting to go higher than had been intended and falling to the earth, 'Where', as the bards had it, 'is the beginning of all living owners of terrestial bodies.' Living beings did not know how to distinguish evil from good and so they had to go down to earth to traverse this sphere till they came back at last to Gwynvyd again. Annwn appears to have had the alternative name of Abred, but in any case it is not easy to remember these Welsh names and they are not necessary to the understanding of the Druidic belief. This, it is clear, much resembled the one built up from the automatic writings. However, in addition, man was believed to have the compulsion to experience every form of existence in order to learn to distinguish good from evil and also to bring this knowledge back to God. This is the real theory of transmigration of souls and appears to be only an extension of the belief in reincarnation. 'Every living and animate being shall traverse the circle of Abred from the depth of Annwn, that is the extreme limits of what is low in every existence endued with life; and they shall ascend higher and higher in the order and graduation of life, until they become man, and then there can be an end of the life of Abred by union with goodness. And in death they shall pass to the circle of Gwynvyd, and the Abred of necessity will end for ever. And there will be no migrating through every form of existence after that, except in the right and liberty of choice united with Gwynvyd, with a view to re-experience and re-seek knowledge.'

The reader will see how closely this bardic theory resembles that of the psychical research communications. Yet here we must observe the time factor. The communications, believed to have been received from Myres are the product of this century. The *Barddas*, from which I have been quoting, were published in 1862. They are said to have been taken from old manuscripts collected in a house which was destroyed by the Roundheads more than two hundred years before this. Whether Myres, who died in 1902, had come across the publications of the Welsh Manuscript Society, I have no means of telling; but even if he had done so in his earthly life, the problem remains of how they could have become restated in automatic scripts. This seems virtually impossible. There appear to be only two alternatives. The first is that these ideas are circulating in the subconscious minds of large numbers of people beneath the religious beliefs which they appear outwardly to hold. The second is that they are genuine attempts to report on an actual state of affairs which it is difficult to describe in words.

Another reason for supposing that the *Barddas* do actually state the Druidic faith is that the classical authors frequently expressed their surprise that the beliefs in Britain and Gaul should be the same as the Pythagorean doctrines found in the Mediterranean. The reader who wishes fuller information should consult Sir Thomas Kendrick's *The Druids*. Caesar (*De Bello Gallico*, Book 6) evidently took a great interest in the subject and for a time had expert knowledge from a Druid Divitiacus, the Æduan, at his headquarters. From Caesar we learn that the purest form of Druidism was to be found in Britain. Students of their lore had to commit great numbers of verses to memory. It is noticeable that a large portion of the *Barddas* is indeed in verse and known as the Triads. There are several versions of the surviving Triads preserved in the *Barddas*. They differ slightly from each other and have the appearance of having been collected in different parts of Wales. No such bulk of material, however, survives as could possibly have taken the twenty years to commit to memory that classical writers claim to have been sometimes necessary. However, what remains appears to contain all the essential details that we need to know.

Since the Pythagorean teaching closely resembled that of the Druids, there is no need to examine it here. However, there has been considerable speculation amongst scholars as to whether Pythagoras obtained his ideas from the Indian sages, who had apparently established some kind of missionary connection with the Near East in his day. It has been suggested also that Druidism reached Gaul and Britain by way of the Greek colonies in southern France. On the whole, however, it seems more likely that Druidism was the accepted belief of the Cwmry when they arrived in Britain about 400 B.C. and that they received no direct teaching from the south. There is no doubt a considerable resemblance between the Brahministic doctrines of India and those of the Druids, but there is also the same degree of resemblance between the older gods of the two areas. Hu and Brahman may be the same concept; but so are Balor and Siva. The art of the Celts derives the origins of some of its patterns from Greece and the Near East, as can be seen demonstrated in Professor Jacobstahl's *Celtic Art*; but these forms had become part of Celtic life long before the Celts of the Iron Age settled in Britain. We may observe and accept the link between the two areas and still not agree that the connecting route lay through the Mediterranean. It seems most unlikely that it did. The route was probably a land one through central Europe and also the time was some centuries earlier than the establishment of the Greek colonies in southern France. It has not been even proved that Brahminism originated in India at all.

Indian religion is so complex in fact that it is improbable that it is by any means completely sorted into its component parts by scholars. Layers of religious thought rest one upon another and are believed to be the result of succeeding waves of conquest by invaders passing into the country. This is certainly true of the well-authenticated invasions by Moslems and is presumably true of the entry of the people known as Aryans. However, if we look at those parts of Hindu religion which are supposedly the result of Aryan immigration and remember that the opinions of scholars vary anywhere between 3000 and 1500 B.C. for the date of this immigration, the thought must cross our minds that there was not one Aryan invasion but several. The picture is like, but even more complicated than, that of western Europe. There is even a resemblance between the general types of the peoples themselves. No religious belief ever seems to have vanished once it became established in India and it never seems to have remained static in the way Christianity and Islam remained static. The beliefs evolve and merge in a most bewildering manner. Even the earliest form of the Aryan beliefs contained in the Veddas, which are thought to have been written in Sanscrit at least 2,500 years ago, give evidence of a combination of faiths at that early time. Conquering races often adopted the gods of the conquered and sometimes turned them into races of demons, who were at times more powerful than their own gods. At other times they accepted them among their own gods. The area of India is so large, has been so frequently invaded and is so remote in thought from our western world, that it is almost impossible for us to form a simple picture, either of its beliefs or of the races which make up its population. The best summary of the religious side of the problem that I have seen is in the recently published *Larousse Encyclopedia of Mythology*. This is not quite what we need for our attempt at comparison, but is very good for the subject as a whole.

At the bottom of the scale are negroid tribes, not unlike the Aborigines of Australia, who are totemistic in belief. They do not concern us except to note that these beliefs seem to have preceded the anthropomorphic all over the world. Higher up the scale come the Dravidians. These Dravidians, a small, dark, long-headed race, have many of the characteristics of the Neolithic people right across the ancient world to western Europe and Britain. It is this type of man who is mistakenly known as a Celt in Wales and Ireland. The Dravidians, akin to peoples in Mesopotamia, were relatively highly civilized. Their ancient cities, such as Mohenjo-Daro and Hrappa, are being explored today. It is believed that they were matriarchal and that their gods were only female. The absence of male gods is improbable, but the goddesses may well have been thought of greater importance. Some of them survived the Aryan invasion and conquest, becoming wives to the gods of the conquerors. Durga and Kali, both of them now considered as wives to the Aryan Siva, are goddesses who once ruled Dravidian life (Fig. 7). Kali has so many points of resemblance to the Mother Goddesses of Britain and Ireland that I feel she must have an identical origin.

The Aryan invaders were organized in three classes, the warriors, priests and ordinary tribesmen, which correspond to those of Ireland in pagan times. In India, where the Aryans made determined efforts to prevent their stock becoming mixed with that of the conquered Dravidians, the three Aryan classes have become rigidly fixed as castes, with a fourth caste of the conquered peoples at the bottom. It is curious that the gods of the warrior caste, the Kshatriyas, although belonging to Brahmanism as a whole, are more or less confined to that caste; while the Brahmanic caste, the priestly one, pays particular devotion to another group. The favourite gods of the Kshatriyas, Indra, Mitra and Varuna, are dated back as long ago as 1400 B.C. on the celebrated tablets of Bogaz-Keui, where they are quoted as witnessing a peace treaty between the Hittites and Mitanni. There they appear less as anthropomorphic gods than as ancestral kings, who had become deified. They resemble in fact such personalities as Woden from whom most Anglo-Saxon kings claimed descent. The semi-mythical Ragnar Lodbrog was on the way to becoming such a god among the pagan Norsemen. Indra much resembles Zeus combined with other Greek deities. Besides his chariot and arrows, he wields a thunderbolt. His chariot becomes the sun and, like Michael, he destroys the great obstructive dragon, Vritra. He represents the benevolent forces of nature and has some resemblance to Hercules and Dagda; but is at a later stage of evolution, perhaps more comparable to Lugh Indra is clearly not a product of Indian soil; although, as bringer of the monsoon to the parched plains, he has developed some qualities in that land. He is the god of conquering warriors, who had evolved him elsewhere. We may be justified in imagining that the story of Michael and Lucifer, or rather Michael and the Old Dragon, originated in the tale of Indra and Vritra and that it may even have been reflected in the Teutonic story of Beowulf and Grendel. Indra is often considered as forming a trinity with Varuna and Mitra, but he appears to be quite distinct. He is in human form and in far-off days may even have lived as a man. Varuna and Mitra scarcely appear in human form; they are counterparts of one another. Mitra is the sun; Varuna the moon. Together they have universal power and protect law, order and right. Mitra was known in Persia; but there his brother, Varuna, was not found. Instead he was associated with the great Persian god, Ahura Mazda. Often spoken of as the 'Knights' in the early Vedic writings, they are also healers. Their parents were the sun and the cloud goddess, but the sun was not Indra. They therefore belonged at one time to a different cycle of beliefs, which can be identified as far west as Rome in the great twin brethren, Castor and Polux. They do not appear to come into our story.

The horse sacrifice and the ritual mating of the rajah's wife to a stallion have been studied earlier in this book, and compared with cases of similar ritual in the British Isles. In the Indian case the stallion represented the sun and the ritual was intended to endow the realm with fecundity. In Donegal in the twelfth century A.D., the same rite was apparently carried out by the king on his installation. Here, however, the king was mated to and had actually to eat a white mare and bathe in a bath of broth made from her meat. This surely means that the rite was older than the Indian one and belonged at one time to a matriarchal phase of society. In this case then it probably came with the Aryans, who had picked it up from the ancestors of tribes who in the Altai, as was noted earlier, still perform horse sacrifice, or did so until the days of photography.

The link with the witch cult here is found in the witch trials published by Margaret Murray. The Devil, in the guise of a horse or other animal, mated with the women of the congregation. Although the object was to ensure the fertility of man and beast, the ritual represented the union of Diana and Pan.

In the case of the King of Donegal and the white mare, which

139

presumably represented the Great Mother as the moon, the positions of the sexes are reversed. In the Indian rite the rajah's wife represented the moon and the stallion the sun. In Gaul, Epona was descended from the union of a man with a mare. This is an earlier phase than that of India, being nearer to the totemic original. The anthropomorphic god had to be mated to the totem beast, who was the mother of the tribe.

This horse marriage rite in India seems to be earlier than the Varuna-Mittra stage; but it may have been part of the Dravidian religion in which Durga and Kali were forms of the Mother Goddess; or, as I suggested before, it may have been imported from a different area. Durga, like Indra, whom she preceded, destroyed a dragon, or rather a demon, and released it in human form. This may be the matriarchal form of the Michael-Indra dragon triumph.

The priestly caste in India had such a complication of beliefs that it is quite impossible to attempt to sort them out in a short section of a book. Brahman was originally a kind of cosmic force, comparable to Hu the Mighty of the Druids. In his original conception he appears to have been not unlike the modern idea of a Cosmic Mind creating everything. He has, however, become anthropomorphic to many Brahmins and is represented as a man with four heads. There were once five; but Siva burnt one of them off by looking at it.

Modern Hindu ascetics by the study of their ancient scriptures and the practice of Yoga, have accepted a faith which corresponds closely with the findings of psychical research and thus has much in common with Druidism. It includes a belief in transmigration and you must kill nothing. Whether this belief is of extreme antiquity and was brought into India with the original Aryan conquerors, is very difficult to say. But it certainly appears as if the main ideas go back at least five hundred years before the birth of Christ, by which time Buddhism became an offshoot from it. Beneath this high Brahministic conception, however, is a welter of belief in anthropomorphic gods and demons, in frightening numbers and with devastating names. Agni, Ignis to the Latin world, the god of fire and wind, is of primary importance and at one time appears to have been a bodiless conception, possibly a variant of Brahma or a thought of Brahma.

Of greater interest to this particular inquiry, however, are

the popular deities belonging really to the lower castes. These
appear later on the stage than the gods of the ancient Vedic
writings; but this does not mean that they are newer ideas. They
are probably rising once more from the ruin of their former
worship. Although in India little seems to be ever lost and the
myths of these gods and demons, from whom they are hard to
distinguish, are much more complete, we can see in this mass of
popular gods a similarity to the beliefs of ancient Ireland as
transcribed particularly in the Ulster cycle. Layer upon layer of
belief exists, each layer probably representing some long-for-
gotten conquest or immigration. Our folk stories in England are
the remains of just the same sequence of beliefs and their confusion is due to similar causes.

We will mention a few of these popular deities for the sake of
comparison, but it would be quite impossible here to do more
than give a hurried glance at a vast subject. Rudra was clearly
not an Aryan god, for he is not permitted to share in their
sacrifice of Soma. He is lord of animals and god of the dead,
which makes us think at once of Nuada and the witches' Lord of
the Underworld. It is interesting too that a horse god, Rudiobos,
was worshipped in ancient Gaul. Rudra and his consort, Prisni,
goddess of the dark, appear to have been a Great Father and
Mother, with the emphasis now on the father.

Siva, the great destroyer and at the same time the bringer of
fertility, is apparently a later version of Rudra and still shares
pride of place with Vishnu in popular belief. Siva was married to
what is evidently a triple Dravidian goddess of destruction,
known as Durga, Parvate and Uma. This triple representation of
a deity is typical also of Gaulish gods. There seems little doubt
that Kali, Mahadevi and other goddesses are just different
names for the same deity. Since Rudra was also accompanied by
the same goddesses, there appears to be little reason for not
assuming that he is identical with Siva. Siva was clearly too a sun
god like Balor at some period, or in one phase, for he burnt up
people with his fiery glance. To us Siva seems hard to distinguish
from a demon; although Durga destroyed a particularly
ferocious one. Siva, however, is credited as being a bringer of
fertility as well as destruction and is represented by the lingam,
phallus, in popular belief. His wife, Mahadevi is represented by
the female yoni symbol. As this symbol is common on rocks in

Scandinavia on which the ships and other symbolic pictures a found, it suggested a link between the two areas to seve modern scholars. These yoni symbols are also found in Scotlar particularly the east, often on sites of the earliest metal age.

Vishnu, the other great popular deity, is very unlike Siv although he assumed many disguises to destroy demon Vishnu is a much more abstract conception. His appearance later than the Vedic literature of the Aryans and he appears belong to a different stratum of society. Vishnu is a solar dei but so apparently is Siva; they can hardly have come from t same stratum. Neither of them is really Aryan and one mu suppose that they originated in different parts of the Dravidi world and have risen to popularity again with the passage of t centuries. Indra and Vishnu defeated the Lord of Darkne Vritra, a theme which we are not dealing with in this book, b which I attempted to trace in Britain in *Gogmagog*. Indra was t sun god of the Aryan warriors and here we appear to find a sta in the merging of their solar gods with those of the Dravidiar Vishnu is a greatly beloved god and quite unlike the murdero Siva.

Vishnu is remarkable for his incarnations. He sleeps for lo periods in some kind of watery heaven and appears at interva on earth in a variety of forms known as avatars. He crossed t Universe in three gigantic strides, thrusting the king of t demons, Bali, into the underworld at the third step. We he see a repetition once again of the Michael and Lucifer, Nuada a Balor, Indra and Vritra theme. Since the name of Balor or Bali common to two of the stories and Balor, or Baal, was clearly sun god before he was relegated to the status of demon, albeit very honest and kindly one, we seem to have one story all ov the ancient world representing the replacement of one conce tion of the sun god by a later and rather more educated on Vishnu appears perhaps as the latest conception of one sun g replacing another. His wife, Lakshmi, was born from the chur ing of the sea, which curious act was performed by both gods a demons together. She is a gentle, loving and beautiful goddes who may be compared with Venus and perhaps the Dor Isis.

Krishna was an avatar of Vishnu, born in human form, who credited with a most remarkable philosophical poem, whi many Europeans must have read, known as the Bhagavad-Gita. This Gita really contains the core of Hindu philosophy. Krishna is both god and man; mankind is eternal, although its earthly bodies die; no human being can ever be killed. The whole of earthly life is in fact a delusion. There is no objection to killing others, or being slain yourself, for, as Krishna explains to his pupil, the prince Ajuna, 'They are dead already.' They are also alive always. As Krishna has many lives in different forms, so have they. The whole thing is very like the Druidic ideas in the *Barddas*.

Hindu religious men through ascetism and the practice of yoga strive to attain a state in which they are in touch with higher levels of existence. The reports of those who have reached this stage are extremely like those supposedly reported by Myres through automatic writing and studied by the Society for Psychical Research. But they also bear some resemblance to another kind of research being carried out today in a more material field. This work is being conducted at Oxford in the De la Warr laboratories and its exponents claim that all growing things are built into a kind of 'blue-print' already existing and formed by a network of intersecting rays. The Hindu yogi have reported that after death, on the next level of existence, human beings can obtain anything they need from the 'blue-prints', which are everywhere around them. The correspondence between these ideas derived by very different methods, the one mechanical and scientific, the other what might be described as psychic, is very remarkable and obviously requires a great deal of study. We seem to be being presented in very different ages and in different parts of the world with a religious theory which is essentially the same and which appears to be the product of something carried by the human mind under abnormal conditions. It does not appear to correspond in any way with the theories of orthodox science, which have themselves reached a kind of impasse in which nobody quite knows what is thought and what is matter. Neither does it seem to agree with current theories of psychology.

The exponents of all these ideas, whether scientific or religious, claim to be able to do things which are not possible by ordinary application of the human mind and body. They work magic, or miracle, which ever you like to call it, by the use of a

143

little studied force, which De la Warr terms 'resonance'. Anyone wishing to study the claims put forward for this study should read Day and De la Warr, *New Worlds Beyond the Atom*.

This may seem a far cry from the witches and their rites and dances, but it is not. This is the clue to what they were, and presumably still are, trying to do. To understand the witch religion, it is necessary to have a working knowledge of these other matters. Whether they are correct or not is no concern of ours in this particular study.

The witches, in their Vangelo, claimed to believe in Aradia, who was the daughter of their two great deities, Diana and Lucifer. She corresponds to the Krishna of the Hindu and would be known to him as an avatar. Jesus Christ to Hindus is also an avatar, that is the descent to earth of a god in human form. If I understand the De la Warr theories correctly, this is considered a possibility in his subject also. He has plotted the ray patterns of a large number of objects, animate and inanimate, and considers that they form a double spiral. He claims that a being on a higher level of existence, whose entity was composed of a much greater number of intersecting rays than anything found on earth, could descend the spiral to a lower level. Presumably it could also return up the spiral again.

The powers promised by Aradia to her devotees are either ones connected with resonance, finding treasure (dowsing) healing diseases and making ugly people beautiful (use of the 'Box'), or are related to such faculties as telepathy and clairvoyance, whose existence has already been proved by scientific methods. As I said before, I have made a limited investigation of dowsing myself and know that it is a fit subject for scientific study, when scientists have educated themselves far enough to realize that it is not a bogus phenomenon.

Resonance appears to be akin both to electricity and magnetism. However, it will not work without some impulse given to it by human body and this has to be tuned in like a wireless set. This presupposes the existence of some as yet unstudied force in the human body, akin both to electricity and magnetism, which act like a self-starter on a car. It is to speed up this force which is the objective of both witches and magicians. It was presumably the way to handle this force which was taught by Jesus to his disciples and which now seems to have been either neglected or forgotten. Confidence in the use of this force was the 'faith' which the disciples found it so hard to retain.

The witches maintain that their nudity is necessary to the generation of the force which they are seeking, the power to work miracles. Since the force has not been studied, we cannot say whether this is true or not. It is, however, interesting to see that, in the newly published Gospel of St. Thomas, one of the sayings of Jesus can be interpreted in this way. 'Jesus said: When you take off your clothing without being ashamed, and take your clothes and put them under your feet as the little children and tread on them, then [shall you behold] the Son of the Living [One] and you shall not fear.' Whatever the validity of the belief may be, it is also held by numbers of holy men in India and, according to Pliny, was practised in Britain in his day. Pliny stated that British women went to their religious ceremonies naked and painted black.

Apparently the belief that power could be obtained by stepping up the current in human bodies is very old indeed. The stone circles, which are usually thought to be temples of some kind, are more probably places where violent dancing in a ring took place to engender power, much in the same way as in electricity a moving coil generates power. The stones were probably put there with the idea of containing the power once it had been generated. The idea of generating this power was, in the first case, to compel the sun and moon to continue to bring the seasons. This, I think, is the reason at the back of the witches' ring dances. Any orgiastic practices which resulted were due not to the ceremony itself, but to the general excitement which it caused; although in themselves they would not have seemed wrong to the priests in charge, for they would be thought obviously to encourage fertility by sympathetic magic. Once you have mastered the secret of controlling the power of resonance, of course, the promise of Aradia to the witches that they would be able to bless or curse with it follows naturally.

I am not saying that the witches could necessarily produce any power at all; but the sadhus of India not only believe that they can produce power to move people and objects; they believe that, when they are really skilled, they can reduce their body at will to its component atoms, transport these to a distant place and reassemble them there. The stories of witches flying through keyholes are presumably due to their having entertained similar beliefs. We remember that Jesus taught his disciples the same thing. If they had enough faith they could order a mountain to be removed and cast into the sea and this would be done. It is clear also that the early disciples believed that Ananias and Sapphira were killed by this means. The same belief was evidently held by the early Hebrews, for Moses, in a competition which he won against the priests of Egypt, is said to have turned sticks into snakes. Jesus turned water into wine in the manner promised to the witches.

The witches then had many things in common with other religions and what they believed was not necessarily of a primitive order. It may be said of it that their religion cannot be accepted by orthodox science, but what religion can?

I am not advocating that readers should immediately attempt to join some local coven, if such a thing exists. I am only trying to show that innumerable ancestors of the existing population of western Europe were not such wicked, gullible and ignorant fools as their acceptance of witch beliefs might seem to imply. Edward III, in the eyes of my old pen friend, the late Colonel A. Burne, author of *The Crecy War*, was one of the ablest soldiers ever to command English armies and yet he, according to Margaret Murray, founded an order of chivalry consisting of two covens. At least 50,000 people are said to be descended from Edward III. All these 50,000 people are also descended from Robert the Devil. That is only one line through which witch blood descends. What about the other members of these two covens and all the other covens all over the country? There can scarcely be a soul in the country who has not some of it in him. It is only reasonable therefore to try to see what there was in it which captured their imagination. I feel certain that it had little or nothing to do with eroticism. Was it not that nobody was quite sure, in those days when telescopes were unknown, that the sun and moon would continue to appear in the sky if they stopped encouraging them to do so? It would have been calamitous if the sun and moon had ceased to revolve round the good flat earth. There would have been nothing at all to eat. As far as I can recall, nothing was suggested in Christian doctrine about this important matter, except that at the end the sun would be turned into darkness and the moon into blood. The witch ritual supplied a means for putting off this promised event for as long as possible. And so intelligent people were naturally dualists. It would not be till long after the fall of Constantinople and the release all over the world of more exact information that men would begin to wonder whether all this fuss was necessary. It was the new learning, I think, which killed the witches far quicker than any persecution could have done. Religions seem to thrive on persecution; but you can hardly expect them to do so well on remarks of this kind: 'I say, old man, what do you think you are doing up in the woods, dancing around with all those naked girls?' 'Making the sun turn round the earth of course.' 'But, old chap, hasn't anyone told you yet that it's the earth which goes round the sun?' This astronomical discovery proved very disconcerting to the Christian Church; but it was absolutely devastating to the witches' faith. Its popular reason for existence had gone, and its devotees had to fall back on local matters and attempts to plan with the Lord of the Underworld for their future lives. The coven at some place tried to raise a storm and did not do it—a woman must not whistle, or she might magic up a wind, which the men did not want. The witches at another place tried to kill somebody they disliked. It all became rather trivial, hardly worth being burnt for. It must have been a little difficult to decide what was the best use for the power if they did generate it.

This is, I think, the real reason why we do not know of many witches today. The Church need not take any credit for stamping them out, which it did with the utmost brutality. The credit, if it is credit, goes to men like Copernicus.

Chapter Eleven

NOW that we have collected as much information as is easily found about this religion, the time has come to see what kind of one it seems to have been. For one thing it is evident that it was a composite affair. It was not a single revelation by any means.

As I see it, there was a world-wide belief in a Great Mother and this necessitated a Great Father also. But there were several father candidates available, two of whom were of equal importance. The first of these, as soon as the Great Mother, presumably on account of her observed relationship to the passage of the seasons, was equated with the moon, was the sun. It must have been a little difficult to explain why he was so much brighter than the moon; but a convenient answer was that she produced him in the night, in the same way that children of men and animals appeared. There you have the Diana and Lucifer relationship, Baal and Ashtoreth, Dagda and Macha, or whatever you like to call them.

The second candidate had been conceived in the womb of the Palaeolithic caves. She was the Great Mother of all living things and he was the god of the beasts on which mankind supported itself after they had been born. As time went on his realm came to include the vegetable kingdom also. He was god of the forest, god of the beasts in it and so on; while she was still the Great Mother, Mother Earth. This is the germ of the Diana and Pan love story.

But a third candidate came into being to explain the moon's absence every month. She had gone away on a visit and could not be seen. Where had she gone? As the world was flat and lit by the sun, she had gone out of sight under it, where it must be dark because the earth stopped the light from getting underneath it.

The moon had gone to visit somebody down there, otherwise

they would still see her in the sky. The person she had obviously gone to see was the Lord of that place underneath. She would not go to see anyone down there of lesser importance. The dead obviously went there too. You did not see them any more. They were all down there and the Lord of the Underworld ruled them. From these ideas came such beliefs as that in Tanit's visit to the Lord of the Underworld. An extension of the idea accounted for the alternation of summer and winter. The moon was still in the sky, but when winter came somebody must have gone. This somebody would be the Great Mother's daughter no doubt. A Pluto and Proserpina type of myth came into being.

The modern witch belief, however, seems to belong to an earlier phase than that and it is the Great Mother herself who goes as mistress to the Lord of the Underworld.

Three different beliefs then circulated in the ancient world and parts of each of them became included in the religion of the witches. Just as the popular gods of India are more or less served by the Brahmins, so presumably the popular gods would have been served by the Druidic priesthood. They held a far higher set of ideas themselves; but since the ordinary population paid for their support and their own belief was extremely hard to present to simple minds, they saw to it that the older deities were not left out in the cold. Something of the Druidic belief in transmigration has survived in the modern witch cult. I do not know whether they believe in rebirth in animal form; but their certainly believe in reincarnation. The greater part of they ritual appears to be focused on attempting to persuade the goddess's lover in the underworld to see that they are reborn in pleasing circumstances.

It seems to me to be impossible to substantiate an Old Stone Age origin for the witch cult as a whole. It is a medley of beliefs, which originated in different places. There may be a suggestion, drawn from several small carvings, that there was an idea in Palaeolithic times which might later develop into the worship of the Great Mother, but the idea seems to be weak. On the other hand, there is a body of evidence to suggest that a fully developed belief in this Great Mother was of great antiquity in the Near East. How far back in time this belief originated is unknown; but it would be reasonable to guess that it was not less than five thousand years ago.

The belief seems to have come into Britain in several waves, of which the first hint is in the Neolithic Age, perhaps around 2500 B.C. The evidence is much clearer in the Beaker period, probably some 700 years later, when cup marks on stones in Scottish stone circles apparently represent the yoni symbol of the goddess. In the succeeding Bronze Age, which may have seen the immigration of several peoples, the religion evidently became widespread and stone circles, for the performance of magic-producing dances, are found all over much of the land right up to the islands in the north. We may perhaps conclude that much of the south of Britain was under the sway of one great matriarchal ruler, who had trade relations with countries at great distances away. Crete and Spain, Palestine and Egypt do not appear to have been utterly unknown lands in 1400 B.C. These dates seem now to be subject to a possible error of nearly a thousand years.

After a climatic deterioration in north-western Europe, about 700 years later, another movement began from the Continent to Britain. It seems probable that by 400 B.C. a second large wave of Mother Goddess worshipping Celts was becoming firmly established in England. These were reinforced by the immigration of Gaulish charioteers some two hundred years afterwards. These I take to be the immigrants whose ideas on matriarchy were already shaken. We should perhaps see them as the people to whom Lugh, Nuada and the more sophisticated gods were of greater importance than the primitive concepts of Balor, Dagda, Danu, Macha, Magog and the rest. The Belgae, whose immigration began about a hundred years later still, seem to have been entirely patriarchal.

It is improbable that we can form any opinion as to which group of immigrants introduced the Pan concept; but one of them must have done so, since Jacks in the Green, Robin Hoods and other forms of the Celtic Esus are very common in England. When we remember that practically no literature appears to have survived from pre-Roman England and how relatively uncertain the story told by archaeology is, we can see that most of our reconstruction is no more than informed guesswork. We have no idea, within a thousand, or even two thousand years, of the date of the arrival of the Isis type of Mother Goddess around our coasts. It may have come without any change of population,

150

carried entirely by seamen and passed from port to port the whole way round from the eastern Mediterranean. It was here in Bronze Age times, for a wooden model of a boat, with gold sun discs on the sides, from Caergwyle in Wales, probably dates about 1400 B.C. and these sun discs are characteristically associated with the ship pictures of the Bronze Age in southern Scandinavia. This boat has Isis's eyes on the bows. We have, however, no evidence that this Isis idea was absorbed into the witch religion. Isis is the same Great Mother, with her ten thousand names; but the witches may have had no truck with seamen. There is not the slightest hint that anything to do with boats was ever to be found in their ritual. I prefer to think that seamen were too sensible to believe that they could have any effect on the behaviour of the sun and moon by dancing in the nude on the poop. To them the elements were too close at hand for more to be done than humbly beg for safety and success. Yet as it is fishermen who keep alive certain ceremonies linking the Great Mother and horses, we cannot be sure that they did not share in the beliefs of the landsmen. All cultivation of the soil remained in the hands of Breton women for a long time and the husbands would probably have to take their part in obtaining fertility for man and beast. In the West Country of Britain customs did not differ greatly from those of Britanny. Classical writers recall the existence of island priestesses, who worked oracles for the men of the sea, suggesting that matriarchal ideas obtained for a long time among seamen, even if surviving marine superstitions did not tell the same story.

Magic was the great object to be obtained through the witch ritual and their way to obtain it was by the simple expedient of working up mass excitement. Their aims and the promises given to them by their avatar do not appear to have differed greatly from those of most pagan beliefs and their ritual feasts were common to many including Christianity and Mithraism. The resemblance between their feast and the Christian one is so close as to suggest a common origin for both.

Taken as a whole then the witch cult, the worship of Diana, was by no means the simple survival of a very primitive religion. It was one which gathered ideas round it like a snowball. What remains of it is obviously the palest ghost of the thing it once was. Its enemies have clearly made the most of the opportunities given to them in the trials to blacken it more than it need have been blackened. It would not have seemed in the least out of place in Rome, where doubtless it was perfectly well known. Its aims and beliefs were quite reasonable until it was persecuted. Then, of course, its devotees felt justified in turning to such black magic as they were capable of working against their enemies. We do not hear much of their success. Kipling expressed the whole thing perfectly when he wrote: 'Oh, do not tell the priest our plight, or he would call it a sin; but we have been out in the woods all night a conjuring summer in.' That is what they tried to do. There seems to be no reason why we should think unkindly of them.

Perhaps the most interesting thing which comes out of this investigation is the obvious parallel, drawn not once, but several times, between the beliefs of western Europe and those of India. The scholars of the last generation saw this more clearly than people do today. I am thinking in particular of the late Sir Flinders Petrie, who suggested that the link was through the movements of the Aryans. The term Aryan is under a cloud nowadays, which seems rather unfortunate, for it denoted a real migrating race of conquerors. It is generally thought that the Aryans, a word which means 'noble', came from southern Russia and then gave their name 'Iran' to Persia, before emerging on the plains of India. This may be so; but I doubt it. I think the Aryans came from hill country, because their calendar appears to have been based on movements up from valleys into the hills, for the summer months, and back again. I should be more ready to look for their origins at the foothills of some mountain mass. It could be the Caucasus, of course, or it could be Asia Minor. Their language when they reached Persia was almost the same as the Vedic tongue of early India. Some regard it as the ancestor of most of the tongues of western Europe.

If we are right in thinking that waves of migrations spread out from a common centre and reached western Europe as well as India, it explains the similarity in the names and characteristics of Celtic and Indian gods. It explains also why Ireland was known as Eire, or something closely resembling it, at least three hundred years before the birth of Christ. Ireland, just as much as Iran, or Eran, was a land of the Aryans. I like this. The men of

152

the Ulster story were 'nobles' right enough. Surely the picture of Cuchulain driving shouting at the men of Connacht, alone with Laeg, his red-headed charioteer, and the straining horses, is about as dramatic an illustration of the Aryan noble as anyone could wish. It is far better than anything India or Persia can produce. Now that Sir Cyril Fox has reconstructed the chariots, put enamelled brooches on their horse blankets and great phalloi on their poles; when we have seen their spears and long slashing swords ourselves, we can appreciate the men of the Celtic Iron Age as nobody has been able to do for two thousand years. Like Caesar long ago, we can grasp something of the wild excitement of it all. All the strands have to be collected, and woven once again into their pattern, before the old world, with its weird beliefs and strangely beautiful art, its heroes and its gods, leaps at us from out of the mists of Time. Oh, I know Lord Raglan has suggested that Cuchulain was nothing but an idol, but what of that? This is how the Irish warriors behaved, or no bard could ever have described it.

Although, as we have, I hope, seen, the Aryan part in this story is clear, we must not forget the Scythians of the Plains. They are probably responsible for the great part played by the veneration of the horse in the ancient story of western Europe. They do not appear to have used the war chariot; but they certainly had wagons. Their sacrificial customs seem to have been adopted both by the Celtic peoples and the Aryan invaders of India. Herodotus tells us that their kings claimed descent from gods, who he identifies with Zeus and Hestia. Although it seems improbable that his identification was correct, for Zeus is intimately connected with the oak forests and Hestia with the domestic hearth of settled life. The Scythians were nomads. Nevertheless the horse's head ornaments which begin to appear in the Late Bronze Age of western Europe, and the innumerable horses' heads which are found on the brooches of pagan Anglo-Saxon England, were probably derived from contacts with the Scythians. They owe nothing to the classical world. The late Professor Bury was of the opinion that the Anglo-Saxons, who came into Britain in late Roman times, were east German tribes and not the descendants of those tribes known to Tacitus and other classical writers. I do not think that this view is necessarily correct, for I can see many pointers, particularly in their pottery,

153

to an origin in North Germany and Denmark; but if it is partially correct, then contact with Scythia is easily explained.

It will be many years before problems of this kind are completely solved; largely because so few archaeologists in Britain can be bothered to tackle so difficult a subject. The earlier periods of prehistory are relatively easy; there are few contacts with other lands. As time goes on, however, the study becomes increasingly complicated, with seaborne influences coming in from all directions. I have only seen two books on Scythian art and archaeology produced in Britain in the last generation. How can we study this matter till more is done?

One thing seems to me to stand out clearly from all we have attempted to investigate in this book. The witch religion, the Dianic Cult if you like, was compounded from several different beliefs. It was added to through the ages to such an extent that it is now difficult to sort them into their component parts. However it was not just one belief out of many. It was the only real belief of the people as a whole, generation after generation, from the Early Bronze Age to the coming of Christianity. Even after this, it remained as a substratum until improved knowledge of astronomy and geography showed men that their ideas of the functions of sun and moon were not like those which their religion had been designed to influence.

All ritual in every religion is a form of magic. It is performed in an attempt to persuade some god or other to do something for the people concerned. For thousands of years the peoples of most of the world performed a ritual for one main purpose. They wished to persuade the moon and sun to continue their work of ensuring the fertility of man, beast and field. For this the sun and moon had to be badgered into returning in their courses round the earth, so that summer and winter did not cease; seed time nor harvest fail. The stone rings on our hills and the wild dances of the witches were all designed for this great purpose. All over the ancient world it was the same. The magic power was generated, or so it was thought, by these dances, and it was kept in and directed to its object by the stone circles, which were put there so that the power should not drift away and be lost in the countryside. Men and women were persecuted and burnt for doing what seemed to them to be an entirely necessary action. If they stopped, the seasons would not return. There would be nothing to eat. Better that some of them should be sacrificed for the good of everybody they thought, and they were willing to do it. Then suddenly, like one of the Cailleach's own thunderbolts, it was learnt beyond any possibility of doubt that it was all in vain. The whole idea was wrong. The earth went round the sun and the moon round the earth. How could anyone believe in the magic any more? The moon was a tuppeny-ha'penny little thing and the sun unapproachable. No wonder the remnant of believers, who clung grimly to their old beliefs, concentrated on a Lord of the Underworld. Who knew? He might still exist.

Index

157

160

Valkyries, 83
Vangelo, *see* Gospel (Witch)
Varuna, 126, 138, 139, 140
Veddas, 137, 141, 142, 152
Venus, 22, 142
Vishnu, 72, 142

Wales, Welsh, 29, 46, 57, 65, 67,
    112, 119, 134, 136, 138
Wandlebury, 84, 85, 88, 89, 91,
    92, 93, 94, 119, 127. Fig. 9, 12
Water Divining, *see* Dowsing

Wat Tyler, *see* Peasants' Revolt
Wheeler, Sir M., 67, 81
Whittlesford, 83–6, 87, 88, 89
William, Duke, 62, 87. Fig. 5, 1
William, Rufus, 87
Wine, *see* Feast
Witch Cult, 2, 3, 5, 7, 10, 24, 26,
    35, 41, 61, 74, 119
Wolf, 106

Zeus, 19, 102, 138, 153
Zoroaster, 4, 9